BEYOND
THE
DIRECTOR'S
CHAIR

10 Leadership Success Strategies for Aspiring Directors

LEAH RIFKIN

Beyond The Director's Chair
10 Leadership Success Strategies for Aspiring Directors

Copyright © 2017 by Leah Rifkin. All rights reserved.

No part of this book may be reproduced, transmitted, or distributed in any form or by any means, electronic, mechanical, photocopying, recording, scanning, or otherwise, without the prior written permission of the author.

ISBN: 978-1-77277-116-9

Requests to the publisher should be addressed to:

10-10-10 Publishing
Markham, Ontario

For Mr. Hosios, for being the first person who showed me that I could be an amazing director and leader.

TABLE OF CONTENTS

Foreword 1
Acknowledgements 3
Introduction 5

Chapter 1: Know Thyself 10
    Interview: Jamie Babbit 20

Chapter 2: Come Prepared 28
    Interview: Jordan Roberts 38

Chapter 3: Command The Room 47
    Interview: Gail Harvey 56

Chapter 4: Exude Positive Energy 59
    Interview: Stefan Brogren 67

Chapter 5: Be Responsible 78
    Interview: Paul Saltzman 86

Chapter 6: Connect and Understand 100
    Interview: Spencer Maybee 110

Chapter 7: Take on Challenges 124
    Interview: Ken Girotti 134

Chapter 8: Communicate Your Vision 152
    Interview: Yannick Bisson 163

Chapter 9: Collaborate and Listen 167
    Interview: Paul Gross 177

Chapter 10: Motivate and Inspire 182
    Interview: Norman Buckley 191

Afterword 197

About the Author 198

FOREWORD

WHEN LEAH ASKED ME to write the Foreword for her book, I was so thrilled! As a leader in the business world I know how important leadership skills are to being successful in every field.

Storytelling is such a big part of all of our lives and as a spectator of cinema and television, you rarely think about all the hard work that goes into making the films and television shows you love.

Through reading *Beyond The Director's Chair* I have learned that being a director is very similar to being an entrepreneur and coach, both in which I have ample years of experience. At its core directing is really the management of people, the communication of a vision or ideal goal, and the handling of problems.

The strategies outlined in the book are easy for you to follow and understand and can be implemented and practiced in your own life. The beauty within these pages is the strategies that are detailed in each chapter can be applied to anyone who has to take on a leadership position, even if you aren't a director or in the entertainment industry. Leadership is a skill that you can learn and improve upon if you are willing.

This book gives you, as an aspiring director, a road map to taking on any project and confidently leading your production team. The interviews in each chapter provide another viewpoint for you to consider, which gives aspiring directors new ways to look at the strategies explained in the chapters. In addition, the interviews add another layer to the already valuable content that Leah provides in the book.

Beyond The Director's Chair should be a standard reading material for aspiring directors and film students. I would recommend that you read this book, if not to learn something new, then to at least improve your leadership skills and apply the new leadership techniques you will learn on your next project.

Raymond Aaron
New York Times Bestselling Author

ACKNOWLEDGEMENTS

AS A DIRECTOR I know that I cannot do my job without the support and hard work of the crew and cast that I work with. Similarly, I could not have completed this book without the help and encouragement of amazing people who surround me.

- I thank all of my fellow directors who took the time out of their busy schedules to do an interview for the book: Jamie Babbit, Yannick Bisson, Stefan Brogren, Norman Buckley, Ken Girotti, Paul Gross, Gail Harvey, Spencer Maybee, Jordan Roberts, Paul Saltzman, and Yael Staav.
- I thank Raymond Aaron for writing the Foreword to my book and for his guidance every step of the way.
- I thank Alexandra Jundler, for her assistance in editing the manuscript.
- I thank my father, Louis Rifkin, for reading through my draft and for his thoughts and opinions. I also thank him for his ongoing love and support of me and my goals.
- I thank my mother, Oretta Rifkin, for her ever-flowing love of me and her much needed words of wisdom and encouragement throughout this journey.

- I thank my partner in life, Edan Kelner, for his unconditional love and his constant validation of my abilities as a director and as a leader. I would not be where I am today without his kindness and support.
- I thank my brother, Shimon Rifkin, for his belief and his trust in me.
- I thank my cousin, Nicky Phillips, and my aunt, Susan Phillips, for always being sources of inspiration to achieve my dreams.
- I thank my cousin, Lisa Phillips, for always seeing the best in me and for giving me many opportunities to grow my leadership skills while working at her camp during the summer. I also thank her for helping me layout the book.
- I thank my mentor, Meir Ezra, for his continued support of me and my work as an entrepreneur and filmmaker.
- I thank my assistant, Laura McCallum, for helping me with research for the interviews and promotion for the book.
- I thank my book designer, Ryan Anderson, for all his hard work and efforts on making my vision for this book come true.
- I thank Vikki for helping with the design ideas for the front and back covers of the book.
- I thank Dennis Lieu for his help fixing the cover designs.
- I thank thank my friend, Ash Walani, for his input for improving the front cover.
- I thank all of the crew and cast with whom I have worked with over the years. Our experiences together have taught me so much about what it means to be a great leader and you have all been my inspiration for this book.

INTRODUCTION

TO BE A SUCCESSFUL leader in the entertainment industry, especially if you're in the role of a director, it is important to accept the responsibility that comes with the role. People are relying on you as the director to be a leader, give direction (pun intended), and keep the production on track.

Before we get into the meat and potatoes of the book, I think it would be good to provide you with a bit of background on how I got started with directing.

My journey began when I was quite young. When I was about 12 years old, I decided that I wanted to try my hand at an acting career. I did some training and started the process of getting an agent. I can't quite remember where things went south, but they did. After a while, I realized that I wasn't putting much effort into it, which I took to mean that I was not particularly passionate about it. I did know that I wanted to be in the arts though. I had been involved with dance since I was 10 years old so I thought about dance as a possible career for a while. The same thing happened where I realized that dance was more of a hobby.

By high school, I had a strong interest in getting involved in the theatre performances. I auditioned in Grade 9 and 10 but did not get cast in a play until Grade 11. It was such a fun experience and I knew that I wanted to direct a play in my last year. I participated in drama classes over the years which taught me about acting, blocking, lighting, staging, costumes, make-up, analyzing scripts, and of course, Shakespeare.

These skills came in handy when I directed my first production in Grade 12. It was a full length play that my co-director and I condensed into a one-act play. *Chamber Music* is about eight ladies in an insane asylum who think that they are famous women in history, including Queen Isabella, Amelia Earhart, Joan of Arc, and others. The story provided a challenge for the actors and my co-director and I. It was tough to block because the majority of the time they were talking with no action so we had to add some in. There was a fun sequence to block where some of the characters were chasing each other and end up choking one character to death, then they all go nuts; some start climbing up on tables, one starts ripping up paper thinking it's snow, and another sings and dances to opera music. Making that section both somber and comedic turned out to be an interesting challenge.

My time working on *Chamber Music* helped me decide that I wanted to direct the spring play as well. This time it would be a full length play and I told my co-directors that I was hellbent on choosing one that had an amazing script. *The Dining Room* was approved as the play of choice. Without going into too much detail, the play took place in a dining room with different characters in different times, and all the scenes were intertwined. This provided even more of a blocking challenge as there were sometimes two separate scenes on stage at the same time. Looking back on that experience, I gained a lot of knowledge about myself as a director. I learned that I can be picky, that I always push to get the best performance possible from actors, and that I love to laugh during rehearsals because it helps ease the stress. I had so much fun working on that production that it really got me thinking seriously about a career in directing. When the time came to apply to university, I decided to apply for film and television programs.

Jumping ahead a few months, I got rejected from the film program at York University, but got into the film program at Ryerson University in Toronto and got early acceptance to the RTA: School of Media at Ryerson. The choice was difficult, but I ended up choosing RTA because of its reputation and because I would have the opportunity to learn a broad range of subjects. I am unbelievably happy that I decided to choose RTA as it gave me confidence in my abilities as a leader and it taught me a lot about directing and producing. Most of my learning in the program was through 'doing' which helped me when I first began my journey as an entrepreneur.

In my second year I directed a short that was written by one of my peers. We had such a blast working on it and it inspired me to create more original content, which I didn't get to consider again until my last year. In my fourth year, my peer, Wil Noack, and I came up with a web series concept and so the development of *Out Of Frame* began. Within two short months we were already writing episodes and putting together a production schedule. It all came together quite seamlessly and the entire production process was a huge learning lesson for everyone involved. Being that it was my first legitimate production under the name of my business, there were more than a few kinks along the way. I knew that I could improve a lot for the production of Season 2, and I did. My work as a director on *Out Of Frame* taught me a lot about producing and directing content on a low budget. Luckily all the hard work paid off because it won Best Edutainment Series at the 2014 Miami Web Festival and Best in Education at the 2015 Buffer Festival.

I have found that working as a producer gives me more opportunities to be a director. It also gives me more freedom to do what I want since I'm also the one dealing with the business and financing side of a production. Although I do want to branch out to direct more projects created and produced by others.

I wanted to write a book so that aspiring directors could learn leadership lessons early on. There are so many books about directing, but I hadn't found one that really delved deeply into the leadership skills required for such a demanding role. The strategies that I outline in this book are ones that I wish I knew when I first decided that I wanted to be a director.

My hope is that once you're done reading this book you will have a better sense of some of the leadership skills that become an asset as a director. I did not want the entire book to only include examples of my own experiences. I wanted to reach out to other directors who have had different experiences and who could shed more light on each of the subjects.

In each chapter, I've included an interview with a director whose expertise and experience will broaden your knowledge and open your mind. Each director that I spoke to had fascinating stories to tell that teach valuable lessons about being a good leader.

I find it helpful to learn from other people's experiences because it teaches me what to do and what *not* to do. It is a valuable tool on the journey of career development. My goal is to give you some insight into how to communicate your vision clearly and effectively so that it is conveyed with authenticity on screen. Use the strategies outlined in this book as a guide for your directing journey.

1
KNOW THYSELF

SO YOU WANT TO be a director. That's amazing! If it's your passion and you really love it, then that's half the equation. Before you can say that you are (INSERT YOUR NAME HERE): Director - the first question you should ask is...Who are you (INSERT YOUR NAME HERE) as an individual?

> "The only person who has artistic control is the director, and 'director' is how you spell God in Hollywood."
> - **Tom Clancy**

It may sound like a cliché question that is the central theme to most teen flicks that involve a character's self-discovery, but it's actually very important to know. It's more than just knowing what your name and interests are. It's about knowing what your values and beliefs are. You're probably wondering what your values and beliefs have to do with your ability to be a strong director, but they play a huge role in the decisions you make. Below I've laid out a situation where those characteristics will come into play.

Situation: You are on set where a crew member did something that was not very ethical by most standards. This crew member thought that it would be okay to make sexual remarks to an underage actor. Let's say the actor was 16 years old, so not considered an adult by most governments. This actor was professional and dealt with the come-on very politely, but the crew member got physical behind closed doors. The actor is now very distracted on set and cannot seem to get through a scene without feeling a little shaken up.

You notice that something is wrong and decide to take the actor aside to ask about it. She reluctantly tells you what happened, tears rolling down her face. She explains that the crew member who assaulted her said that she "looks very pretty in a mini-skirt and should wear them more often" and then touched the small of her back when no one could see.

Now, some people may not see this as a terrible thing. Some may even tell this actor to take it as a compliment. However, clearly the actions of this crew member have upset the young actor and have affected the way she can do her job.

For that actor, the actions of the crew member were definitely considered harassment. As the director you have to ask yourself: What do you consider harassment? Where do you draw the line? You have to bring in all the facts as well as your own personal beliefs and values regarding assault and harassment. A highly ethical production team would have policies put in place when it comes to these kinds of situations, but at the end of the day, you have the power to make the situation better. What would you do in this situation? Which of the possible outcomes below would you choose?

Do you:

1. Reassure the actor that the crew member's behaviour was a compliment to her beauty and that she shouldn't look into it more than what it was.

2. Reassure the actor that the crew member's behaviour was highly inappropriate and unprofessional and that you will ensure that the crew member does not do it again.

3. Decide then and there that the crew member is terrible and immediately fire the crew member in front of everyone on set.

4. Give the crew member a warning and remind him/her of the consequences if it happens again.

5. Take the actor and the crew member in question aside to discuss what happened further. You want to understand both sides of the story then decide the appropriate actions to take.

6. Do nothing and get on with the production. Time is money.

7. Do a combination of some of the above options.

8. Do something that was not listed above.

In delicate situations such as the one described above, as well as in any situation that involves other people, it is always important to remember the rights that all involved parties have, whether you agree with their behaviour or not.

Know Thyself

I strongly recommend understanding a situation in its most factual form; what happened, who did what, what was said, how was it handled, etc., before making an executive decision. It is going to be your values and beliefs that make you decide to deal with the situation one way over another. It's not about taking sides, it's about considering what you believe to be right or wrong, and making sure that you are applying what you believe to be the best solution.

Things like values and beliefs have a lot of grey areas because they are different for everyone, which is why it is important that you know yourself and what you stand for. You are the leader and you need to make decisions, even the hard ones.

> "It was always my dream to be a director. A lot of it had to do with controlling my own destiny, because as a young actor you feel at everyone's disposal. But I wanted to become a leader in the business."
> **- Ron Howard**

The next thing you need to know is your directing style. This is not a book to tell you *how* to direct. It's a book about how to be a good leader as a director. Your style is your own. Some directors are more assertive, some are more inclusive in their decisions, and some are quite reserved and soft-spoken. There are certain things you can do so that you present yourself as a stronger leader, but we'll get to those in the later chapters. It comes down to knowing how you like to direct the performers and how you manage the crew.

PAY ATTENTION TO THIS NEXT SECTION. This is where many people tend to be less aware and it can often result in bad behaviour and taking out their frustration on other people.

You have to know your limits. To do this, you should ask yourself questions such as the ones below:

What are your pet peeves?
What kind of behaviour pushes your buttons?
What kind of triggers will get you frustrated or angry?
How do you know when you're too tired to continue working?

These are questions that you should ask yourself. I'll tell you a bit about myself to get you thinking and help put it in perspective.

My pet peeves include people showing up late, people being lazy and slacking off rather than putting in 110%, and people who don't take responsibility for their actions, or who blame their actions on others.

Now this isn't to say that I haven't been guilty of those things myself, but I'm not afraid to admit it and say that I was wrong. The behaviour that really pushes my buttons, especially when it comes to life on set, is when people don't respect others. I don't just mean respect in the simplest sense of basic respect for another human's existence on this earth, I mean respect for a person's responsibility and talents. I've seen and heard stories about directors who treat people with 'lesser' jobs terribly. The production assistant may be lower down in the credits, but it doesn't mean that they are less important than the director by any stretch of the imagination. Here is lesson #1 in being a great leader on set:

Respect the jobs of everyone in the production crew as well as the performers. Your vision on screen would not be possible without every single person who helped.

If you can't do that, good luck finding great people to

work with. In my experience most people want to work with other people who are respectful of everyone on the team. Everyone doesn't have to be best friends and hug one another at the end of the day, even though that would be awesome, but respecting one another's responsibilities and talents is key.

This also comes into play as a director because you should know and understand every crew member's role. You don't have to be an expert, but you should be able to communicate differently with crew depending on what they do on set. Not only will you be more effective in your overall communication, but you'll also gain a ton of respect from the people around you. Of course, the bigger the production, the more people, so there will be a greater variety of roles. It should be a goal to have a detailed understanding of all the production roles. It will require hours of research and many different experiences on a variety of productions. Are you willing to put in the work? Take a moment and think about how much effort you would put in to be the best director you can be. You can even go as far as to write out a comprehensive list of the things you need to do to get there.

One limit you should be highly aware of is your energy levels. When it comes to knowing when I am tired, it usually is quite obvious when I am pushing so hard that I don't eat or drink, or even go to the bathroom, and then I start getting snappy and become a bit of an extreme perfectionist. I'm a perfectionist in general, but it just becomes ridiculous and unreasonable. Then it's pretty much downhill from there. I don't remember the experience that made me realize that.

I do know that the rule about always feeding my crew

applies to me as well. Now when I am on set, I make sure to find the time to eat (even if it's half a sandwich or a bit of fruit), drink water (I try to finish the equivalent of at least one water bottle), and use the washroom (at least once if it's an 8 hour shoot). It might sound ridiculous but I can tell you now that it's a great quality to know about yourself. Handling your own energy can be done in three easy steps:

1. Recognize when your behaviour begins to change because of your energy levels.

2. Figure out what is causing it (i.e.: lack of sleep, dehydration, hunger, etc.).

3. Implement the solution (i.e.: take a 5 minute cat nap, grab a fresh water bottle, take a break to have a healthy snack, etc.).

The last suggestion that I have is to know your expectations of yourself and others. What can others expect of you as a director and as a leader? What do you expect of your crew and actors?

All of these elements that go into knowing yourself are a major part of being a great leader. They all come down to one question: What is your message? In other words, what do you want people to think of you? What first impression do you give?

A great way to know what impression you give to people you work with is to ask them. It's a lot easier than you think it may be, you just have to be willing to hear what people have to say. Think of it as an opportunity to grow and become a better you!

Before you keep reading, please take some time to write out your answers to the following questions:

What can others expect of you as a director and as a leader?
What do you expect of your crew and actors?
What is your message?

Be very honest with yourself and confront who you are as a person. Trust me when I say that it will save you from finding out the hard and less private way. This is an introspective process and you don't really want to be finding out these things in a stressful situation during production.

SELF-DISCOVERY

I've had several moments of self-discovery while directing but there are two moments in particular that stand out to me. On set of the test shoot for *Revolution 10*, an interactive feature film that I'm directing, I realized that I had much more to learn and that I had to do more research and increase my knowledge on the other aspects of filmmaking. I knew I had to learn more about the protocol on set and the terms that should be used on set.

I had another moment at the end of the finale shoot for *Out Of Frame* in the second season. I didn't realize it while it was happening, but I recognized afterwards that by being a decisive leader I was able to make sure that I got the footage that I needed in a short amount of time. While I was reviewing the footage over the next few days, I realized the amazing thing that had been accomplished. I realized that I did a really good job at executing my vision and was super proud of myself.

Once I directed a music video and the camera assistant noticed that one person had been looking into the camera on occasion. I decided to make an announcement to remind the performers not to look at the camera even though the note only applied to one person in particular. Instead of calling that person out I made the statement to the whole group. The 1st Assistant Camera actually said that I did the right thing and acknowledged that that was why he wasn't the director. I recognized that I was being a good leader and in the moment made the best decision for the good of the group.

MY MESSAGE

I want people who I work with to want to work with me again, otherwise what is the point? I can't do what I do without the people around me so I always make sure that I am being the best version of myself on set. When someone says that they had fun on a project and ask to keep them in the loop about any further projects then I succeeded. I did my job of being a leader well.

The way I see it is if everyone on a project has fun and works hard, they can be proud of the end result. Yes, this industry continues to grow because of all the sales and distribution of content, but it's also due to admirable integrity and creativity of talented media professionals. A successful film or television show is the masterpiece of everyone involved, not just of the director, the executive producers, or the actors.

My directing style is simple. My style is hard work. It is expressing my vision with clarity. My style is to be respectful to everyone involved and being grateful for the opportunity to show my talents. My directing style is leadership.

I'll close off this chapter with one more question: If you don't know who you are, how can you have vision?

It's much more difficult to bring a script to life without being your most authentic self because then you're not going to be in the moment on set and you're definitely not going to earn the full respect of the people around you. The odd part is that you can learn so much more about yourself while directing a project. I find that having a basis or a starting point makes the learning and growing much more enjoyable and more advantageous. By knowing who I am and what my ethics and values are then the continuous process of self-development is much easier to navigate and understand.

> "Directing is so interesting. You know, it just sort of encompasses everything that you see, that you know, that you've felt, that you have observed."
> **- Barbra Streisand**

INTERVIEW WITH
JAMIE BABBIT

*But I'm a Cheerleader, Gilmore Girls,
Popular, Drop Dead Diva, Girls*

When and how did you discover that you wanted to be a director?

Well I started as a child actor, so I first got interested in storytelling through acting. I was a child actor at the Cleveland Playhouse doing the plays and I was also on a local television show in Cleveland. So I really loved acting when I was a kid and I was very struck by the depth that you have to deal with in theatre — at the end the play is over and there is no record of it. As a child that really upset me because I would be so depressed after each performance that the whole thing was going to end. There was something that I liked about the TV show that I was on, how that was something that lives on forever. So I very quickly transitioned out of wanting to be in the theatre to wanting to be in film and TV.

When I was in high school, I was still acting in the school plays and I started getting involved backstage and realized I actually liked that better. I started working in lighting and working as the stage manager and realized there was this whole other world outside of acting where everyone was on headsets talking shit about the actors and I was like, "This is much better!". By the time I went to college I was kind of disenfranchised with acting and realized I wanted to go into the behind the scenes.

I went to Barnard College, which is part of Columbia University in New York City and I got an internship with Martin Scorsese on *The Age of Innocence*. I was an office production assistant where basically I would buy gifts for Martin Scorsese's girlfriend, I would go to Martin Scorsese's parent's house and pick up booties that his mom was knitting for Steven Spielberg's new baby, and I would buy peanut butter and jelly for Martin Scorsese's trailer. It was just really menial tasks, but it was a real portal for me into the life of a director.

I worked in the office where he had all of his storyboards for *Raging Bull*, all of his shot plans, and his personal 35mm film collection. He is a real student of film and even being an exceptional filmmaker he still considers himself a student of film. And I thought, "God, I really am a student so I have a lot to learn." He used to do this cool thing, and I'm sure he still does it, where he screens his 35mm films for his cast and crew during filming of whatever current movie he's working on. He will screen movies he loves or shots he loves, or tones of a theme that he loves. He'll screen old movies for the cast and crew to get it into his head and explain where he's going with whatever particular project. So when I was his office PA, I was in charge of organizing film prints and the film screenings that he would have for the cast and crew, especially on *Age of Innocence* with Daniel Day-Lewis, Michelle Pfeiffer and Winona Ryder.

It was a great first job with a director. Even though I never officially met Martin Scorsese, I knew a lot about his day-to-day life just based on doing all of his menial tasks. So I thought, "Wow, this is is really a great job because you will never be good enough. You have so much to learn and that was really exciting for me to throw myself into a field where you would always be challenging yourself, even if you were as famous or successful as Martin Scorsese.

Then I think I was really convinced that I wanted to do that. I got an internship at the Sundance Film Festival. Just hearing about that, I thought maybe that was something I should explore by making an independent film because that seemed like the easiest way into directing. So I went to Sundance as an unpaid volunteer where I was a ticket taker. I was trying to acquire knowledge about how one becomes a director, how one starts, how one gets the money together. It's such a daunting profession so I wanted to get more information. So I started with people who were making movies who were in their twenties. They were all at Sundance and I was like, "How did they get here?"

Through working at Sundance, I realized that people had short films first and then once they had short films, they graduated to feature films. That was my new goal — I needed to make a short film that was really good and get it into Sundance and then I'd use my experience at Sundance to find a financier to make a feature film. So that's what I did. I was working on other people's movies along the way to make money and save money to make my own short film.

I randomly got a job with David Fincher who was directing his movie after *Seven*, his big hit. I met him and his wife at a film festival in L.A. and introduced myself and they said they were looking for crew so I got a job as a script supervisor on Michael Douglas' *The Game*. I saved money from that, and while I was working on that movie I asked David if I could use the leftover 35mm film from *The Game* to make my film, and use his Avid to edit. I also asked Michael Douglas if he would write a letter to Paramount Studios so I could shoot my short film on the studio lot. I basically used that job as a way to get a lot of favours. And so I made my short film *Sleeping Beauty* after that, which did go to Sundance in 1997 I believe.

During the experience of making *Sleeping Beauty* I realized I really loved directing film. It was a 15 minute film, but it was such an exhilarating experience putting the whole thing together. Extremely difficult but very worth while. I was really pleased with the outcome of the movie and I was really hooked for life after that.

What's been the most eye-opening experience of self-discovery while you've been directing over the years? Is there one that stands out in particular?

I think when you make films and tell stories you end up discovering a lot about yourself. I knew that in order to make a successful film, it had to be very personal. In my experience of watching debut features at Sundance, it seemed like the more personal and more specific a movie was to the filmmaker's experience, the more truthful it would be and basically it would just be a better film.

I was very determined for my debut feature to try to make a movie that was as specific to me as possible and to what I was interested in and to what my influences were at the time. I had grown up as part of rehab basically because my mother ran one of the biggest rehabs in Cleveland. It was a drug and alcohol rehab for teenagers. My whole childhood was spent there just because my mother was running it, and she was so busy so she really incorporated her family into her rehab.

I knew I wanted to make a comedy about rehab. I had also come out as a lesbian and I wanted to use all of the feelings that I had about being gay. So it seemed like a perfect intersection of my life, to tell a comedic story about gay rehab.

I always was interested in comedy, I consider myself a funny person, I like weird comedies myself so it seemed like a good territory for me. When I read a lot of articles and researched about gay rehab, specifically Exodus International, which was kind of the biggest gay rehab at the time, I was very fascinated by the idea of being straight or being gay as a construct and gender as a construct. I was reading articles about how if a feminist gay man, even a gay male child, learned how to chop wood then he could become straight and be attracted to women. It just seemed so ridiculous and absurd to me that I had to make a satire about this. It was so funny and ridiculous.

I took a UCLA extension class and wrote the treatment for *But I'm a Cheerleader* and in the process of developing that script and even making *But I'm a Cheerleader*, it really fermented my ideas about who I was, which was a product of being raised in this rehab environment, having a very dry sense of humour about it and also what it was like to be gay at that time.

What is your message? In other words, how do you want people to talk about you? What do you want them to say about you, with regards to you being a person but also a director? What is the message you want people to know about you?

I don't really care what people know about me or think about me. It's not anything I ever think about. What I think about is what kind of art interests me in the moment, what kind of stories interest me. I feel like in order to really be who you are, you have to give up caring about what people think.

How would you describe your directing style?

I would say being a good director is being a good listener and being very in touch with what's going on in the moment. I think my directing style is that I'm very in-tune to what magic is happening right in front of me with the actors, and frankly what magic isn't happening. If a scene is not working, I am confident enough to address it right then and there and am able to fix the scene. I am able to inject it with whatever it needs to keep it going, to make it fly. Because so much about directing is that you're basically a band leader or conductor where if all the musicians are doing the right thing, they just need someone who is waving their wand and keeping everyone on the same tone. But as often is the case, there are some players that are not working and not doing a good job so you have to be able to hide the bad with the good so no one notices. I feel like that is a huge part of directing.

How does knowing who you are influence how you direct and how you approach directing?

You have to know who you are and be confident in who you are in order to be an honest person who can be in the moment. I feel like if you really know who you are and comfortable in your own skin you can inspire the actors to be comfortable in their skin and to take risks, you can inspire the director of photography whose capturing images to be comfortable in who they are. I feel like being a leader and being a director is all about making people feel calm, making people feel safe so they can be the best that they can be. You have no chance of inspiring greatness in other people if you are not comfortable with who you are.

What advice would you have for aspiring directors or up-and-coming directors who aren't feeling confident?

You discover who you are by actually making the art. If you just sit around in your head and don't actually start doing things, you'll get nowhere. The first thing any aspiring director needs to do is to start making films because in the process of making them, you begin to understand what you personally are interested in. I would encourage any director to really trust exactly what they're interested in and pursue that doggedly.

There's so much blandness out there and there are so many people trying to fit in, so everything is the same. The more that a director really discovers who they are, the better, but it happens in the process of doing the art. I don't think any painter thinks to himself, "Who am I? Who am I? Who am

I?" for ten years and then starts to paint. I think you just start painting and then in the process of painting you're like, "Oh I like these colours, I like to paint this kind of thing, I don't like doing landscapes and I'm not interested in that, I'm interested in doing portraits." You learn what you like just by trying things so I just think getting out and doing is the best thing.

Are there any other comments or stories that you think are relevant to the topic of knowing yourself and leadership and directing that you want to add?

I think going into therapy is also helpful for a director or for any artist. I feel like when you're in therapy, you're dealing with yourself. I feel like you are forced to look inwards, and therapy is a good way to investigate yourself in a more intense way than just living your life. So I do think being in therapy is helpful.

I used to always think when I was a kid that I never wanted to be a therapist because my mother was a therapist. But I've realized about ten years into my career as a director that they really inform each other, and I really had a leg up as director very early on because I came from a family of therapists. When you learn how to think about people and why they do what they do, all that stuff is really helpful for storytelling and for directing.

2

COME PREPARED

PART OF YOUR DUTY as a director is to come to set prepared. You need to know exactly what the agenda is every day, and since time is money in this industry it is your responsibility to ensure that you stick to the schedule as best as you can.

Every director has his or her own way of getting prepared. It's up to the individual to know what needs to happen. As an example, I'll tell you what I like to do the day before and the morning of a shoot.

1. Put everything I need on set the next day in one pile close to my bag so that I don't forget anything.

2. Get a good night's sleep (or as much sleep as I can).

3. Wake up with plenty of time to get ready.

4. Eat a big breakfast.

5. Have a hot and tasty cup of coffee.

6. Find the least stressful means of getting to set whether that is driving myself, taking the subway, hopping in a cab, or getting a driver for the duration of the shoot.

That's my process and it might not be for everyone. You have to find the process that works for you. The end goal is to arrive on set feeling calm and ready to take on the day's challenges.

I like to have a 'game plan'. A game plan is whatever I need to do in order to ensure that the shots are completed to my expectations. That might mean spending the first twenty minutes of the day chatting with the cinematographer and the actors to explain the look and feel that I am going for. It helps to make sure that they are all working together to accomplish the style and tone of the scenes.

I have learned that it is important to come with a plan B and plan C in mind in case things change – which they most often will. Either way, the skill of thinking on your feet or improvising, or whatever you want to call it, is vital. Many people find thinking of fast solutions a difficult skill to master. There are many different types of training that you can do to feel more confident with it, though I find that improv classes are the best way to go about it. Not only are they super fun, but they really teach you how to think outside of the box and learn to try new things in order to get the desired result. Most importantly improv teaches you to be open minded because saying 'no' is frowned

> "The fact is, you don't know what directing is until the sun is setting and you've got to get give shots and you're only going to get two."
> **- David Fincher**

upon in most improv exercises. The key is to say 'yes' and roll with it. It's quite similar to when a challenge presents itself on set despite being prepared. You have to accept it, and roll with an idea. If that idea doesn't work then try another one. It's also important to remember that you have people around you to help you. Just because you're the director doesn't mean you have to do everything on your own and be the only voice in the decision making process.

There have been times when I have had plans in mind for shots and they haven't quite worked out the way I imagined so I had to come up with an alternative shot on the spot. Once on a short film shoot I didn't know the final layout of the props in one of the locations, which was crucial to figuring out the blocking so I had to block on the spot and create an updated shot list within a few minutes.

Most often though, I have thought scenes out enough to know what will work and what won't. Since I surround myself with super talented cinematographers and amazing actors, I rarely have a problem with how the scenes play out. When everyone follows the path towards the ultimate goal or vision and brings a unique perspective to the table, magic can truly happen.

There are exceptions too. No matter how prepared you may be, there will always be curve balls on set or in post-production that you will need to handle. I would suggest hiring a very strong key team (producer, cinematographer, audio supervisor, production manager, and 1st AD) who can come up with solutions easily and who is always willing to try something new to make it work. Your team is your safety net when it comes to dealing with curve balls. A good leader will ask for help when needed and is not afraid to admit when he or she messes up or makes a wrong decision.

In any case, it is a good idea to have a check list and/or prep ritual when preparing for a shoot. A check list is fairly straight forward. It is a detailed list of everything you need or need to do before a shoot. This could include printing out the necessary documents, re-reading over the script, contacting the location manager to ensure that the location is ready to go, eating a piece of chocolate, having a glass of wine (or chocolate milk), and getting a good night's sleep (or not). Depending on how you work, your check-list items will vary. Three items I would always include are:

1. Review script material.

2. Make a list of questions you require answers to for the start of the day.

3. Get a good night's sleep. Sleep is more powerful and energizing than you might think, especially during a stressful shooting schedule.

> **– BONUS –**
> Visit **beyondthedirectorschair.com/bookbonus** to download my full pre-shoot checklist.

A prep ritual is something that everyone has, whether they know it or not. For me, I like to do several specific things before a shoot. First, I like to print out documents I need and put them on my clipboard, then I review the script material and add any extra notes (new shots or setups to try if there is time, changing a line, reviewing blocking, etc.), then I like to pack my bags and put everything aside so I can grab it easily the next morning. Lastly, I like to make time to text my team (or at least the writer, producer and actors) and tell them to get excited for the shoot. Then I wind down with a cup of tea, shower, and then hit the sack.

You may not do anything particular, but if you pay attention to your own behaviours you'll probably notice some patterns that you tend to repeat before shoots. Any repeated or common activity is a way for you to feel like you're in control. Have you ever skipped a ritual because you thought you didn't need it or because you were too tired? Then woke up and felt like you have forgotten something?

Exactly. Just do your ritual. It's for your own sanity. There have been a couple of times when I have slacked off, not stuck to my rituals, and said that "I'll just do it in the morning", and have regretted it the moment I stepped onto set. I felt frazzled and less confident as a result.

When I am prepared and have thought of every possible detail that I could think of, I feel much more confident. I'm not perfect and do forget things sometimes but when I know I prepared as best I could, it doesn't bother me so much. I also find that the more prepared and organized I am as the director, the more willing the cast and crew are to step up and take initiative. Everyone around me feels more at ease and confident when I am confident in what I am doing.

I have learned my lesson to be prepared many-a-time.

There was a project I was producing and directing when I didn't prepare my shot list ahead of time. I knew exactly which shots I wanted and they were all in my head. It doesn't really help anyone, even myself, if they are just in my head. The morning of the shoot I was frantically getting everything else ready instead of focusing for thirty minutes and doing the shot list. My excuse was that I wanted to wait for the DP to get to set and chat with him before doing so. This was just a test shoot and I learned very quickly that that was no excuse to not prepare in the same way.

The cinematographer arrived to set and we discussed the shots and I made a few changes to my original plans. He gave me some great suggestions for ways to organize things which was helpful. It was a challenge with this particular shoot because we had to shoot scenes several times with different outcomes, so setups and shots were repeated a lot more than normal. When it came down to marking the shots on the script it got a bit confusing for everyone. I gave everyone the benefit of the doubt because it was the first time we had done a shoot like that. We had to do three times the amount of takes that one would normally do, which was a challenge in stamina for the actors and a challenge in organization for myself and the writers. Considering those factors, everyone did well, and we all learned more about shooting interactive stories. I now know better ways to organize future shoots. The overall lesson here was that I didn't do enough preparation for the test shoot so there were more stumbling blocks than there needed to be. Luckily I had a professional group of people helping so it was quite fun even when we were struggling a bit.

No matter what kind of project you're working on it is best for everyone involved when you come prepared to set. As a matter of fact, it doesn't matter whether it is preproduction, production or post-production; you should always arrive confident and ready to go.

The only time I don't plan every bit of minutia out is when I'm dealing with the performances from actors. I always have a clear idea of how I want the scene to go in terms of the tone, but I always like to let the actors play around and bring their own interpretation to the table. If I don't like something an actor is doing, I'll direct them to realign their performance so that it matches the tone I've set to achieve. Often times I'll prefer a creative decision an actor made that makes the scene stronger and ask them to keep doing it. When that happens, I also like to ask the actor to give me variety so that I have choices in the editing room. It's amazing what they can come up with and it can make a scene so much better than how I imagined it. At the end of the day though, if I don't come prepared with something in mind then things get chaotic on every level, with the crew and especially with the performances.

> "I do not always know what I want, but I do know what I don't want."
> - **Stanley Kubrick**

Coming unprepared for a project has a direct effect on my abilities because it initially affects my overall confidence which then carries over to my effectiveness as a director. So I am a wreck if I don't prepare. I am prone to anxiety if I don't prepare. I know that about myself, so I will always prepare to the point where I know I will feel confident and powerful when I walk on set. Even if I don't have every little detail planned out but I have a clear idea of what I want to do, I am good to go.

I had a shoot for a short two minute script that I had to prepare for. I was shooting in a public park so I knew that I might have to deal with people coming in the shot or having to change the location in the park at the last minute. I had prepared a shot list and some basic storyboards to follow. On the day of, there were upwards of two hundred people in the park, but luckily it didn't get in the way of shooting and getting the shots that I wanted. My plan did have to change slightly since I hadn't rehearsed with the actors so I had to improvise a bit for a couple of shots. Luckily we were running way ahead of schedule because the actors took direction so well and I was able to get additional shots that I hadn't planned for that came into use in the editing suite. That was a rare gift that I took advantage of. Had I not prepared for that shoot, it could have been disastrous because dealing with the insane amount of people in the park could have been so overwhelming to the point where I might have made decisions that would have messed up the look and tone of the scene.

The finale shoot for season two of *Out Of Frame* was the first shoot where I was really pressed for time and had to deal with a large cast and quite a few crew members. I was lucky that every crew member pitched in and took initiative, but I also know that had I not prepared the amount that I did before the shoot and made sure that I was organized and that I knew my plan, it wouldn't have gone the way that it did. Not only did I prepare my own stuff, but I also wrote out a document for each crew member so that they knew exactly what their primary and secondary tasks were that day. I had to make sure that everything would run smoothly and ensuring that the crew were prepared at the start of the day made a world of difference. Everyone walked in with a purpose and a drive to do their job well.

There are some basic steps that you can follow to prepare for a shoot. My number one suggestion would be to re-read the parts of the script that you'll be shooting that day. There might be a detail that you missed that could throw off your shoot schedule if you didn't recognize it. Even the best of us forget or miss things. I also usually like to review my shot list and setups just in case I want to make a change, or simply to make note of an option for blocking so that I don't forget it. I'm big on triple checking everything. I'm one of those people that has everything I need ready the night before. I've had times where I've gotten out of bed to write something down or pack something to be able to fall asleep.

Coming prepared also means being emotionally and physically ready. I would suggest saying some positive affirmations before going to sleep, and in the morning get yourself pumped and excited for the day ahead of you. You could even do a short work out to sweat out any anxiety. Exercise also helps with your overall energy levels. If your energy is low then it will surely seep through the set. Your cast and crew will feed off of you so it's your responsibility to get yourself in the right headspace beforehand.

Since most of the projects I have done until now have been low budget productions and since I have also been the producer on many of those productions, I always made certain to be the first person to arrive on set. I know that won't always be the case on future projects, but I think that being early to my own set shows that I am prepared and excited for the day. Since I don't like it when people arrive past their call time I should set the example and always be early for my call time. I think that a director who comes on time and prepared is communicating to the cast and crew that he or she really cares about that project. I think this is especially important on low budget or independent productions where much of the spirit of the project travels from the top down. Since there tends to be less people working on those kinds of projects, a bad or unorganized start to the day can trickle down very fast.

A director who comes prepared is someone who is organized for the day, has a positive attitude moving forward and is confident about handling any situation that may come up. It's not just about being prepared on the technical end of things (blocking or expectations for the performances), it's about being emotionally and mentally prepared for anything. The director is like the captain of a ship. If the captain doesn't know which way he wants the first mate to steer, then the boat will topple or crash and everyone inside it will go overboard. The only way to avoid that is for the captain to come with a plotted course. The director comes in with a vision for the overall project, and each day should come to set with a prepared daily vision which should be communicated to the crew.

In the next chapter we will discuss more about how a director should present himself or herself. It's one thing to arrive prepared, it's another thing to take what has been prepared and then lead a team.

INTERVIEW WITH
JORDAN ROBERTS

Burn Your Maps

What do you do to prepare for a shoot? What kinds of things do you tend to focus on? Do you ever leave anything up-in-the-air so that decisions are more spontaneous? If so, what do you leave up to spontaneity and why?

Well, as a writer of all the things I've directed, I guess my first preparation is making sure the script is as tight as possible. Because I've only worked on films with limited budgets, wasting any time (and thus money) shooting a scene that won't be in the film is a real shame. That said, you can never — ever — or at least I can't — be sure what will actually make it in the final edit. I was absolutely certain I needed every single scene in the shooting script of the last film I directed. But there are at least 8-12 scenes that didn't make it into the film. And, from my current vantage point, it seems completely obvious that they wouldn't be included. Which brings up that old adage about how we make three movies by the time we're done: The One You Write, The One You Shoot, The One You Edit.

And after making sure to the best of your ability to get the script to its fighting weight, it is imperative that you understand it — at least most of it. On the set there are going to be dozens of people who are there to help you (and the writer if that's not you) bring something into reality. I'm always amazed at the dedication in film artists. They take great care and great pride in fulfilling what's on the page, bringing it to life. But very often they will have questions — sometimes big ones. And nothing will sink morale or eat hours like a director who doesn't understand the story or the ideas behind the story.

Another preparation — and this is by far the most important — is making sure you have cast the film well. This can't be overstated. And, again, the old adage in the movie business, about how casting is 80, or 90 or 95 percent (depending who's talking) of the battle. There's great truth to this. Actors, good ones, are trained to widen their range. And many can play almost anything — or so they like to believe. But we and they often suffer from this misconception that anyone can play anyone. The words on a page of a script are merely indicators of what the actor will do. Actors bring the rest. They literally bring the 'life'. As we all know saying the words and doing the actions listed isn't going to get you there. Though that itself is very difficult. What I look for in an actor is someone that does — or will — come to know that human being, that character, better than I do. Someone that will surprise me. Someone that I can let alone to do their work.

Obviously the job of the director is to focus the performance, to keep your eyes and ears open at all times to make sure the actor is inhabiting the character as you see it. But it is a far more satisfying experience to watch a great actor — even a very good one — discover and become fully alive within a character.

As for the value of leaving a few things up in the air, I'm a big believer. But even when I prepare, I'm relying on the likelihood that the 'plan' will get thrown out. At least some of the time. But there is enormous anxiety reduction to be had in having the plan anyway. Shot lists or even early pre-blocking sketches are tremendously helpful (assuming you're working with actors that are comfortable with a director working these things out in advance; some actors prefer and even insist on being a part of how the scene moves.) Again, it doesn't matter if you get to the set and throw them out. You have them. And they are a fall-back in the event that the day goes to hell, or you haven't slept in 24 hours and don't have a decent idea, or if any number of other things that can go wrong do go wrong.

One thing we are usually best NOT planning is how we think a line should sound, how it should be read. This is especially true as writers. You've written the script and rewritten it a hundred times (hopefully!), but now it's time to let an actor make it alive. Giving line readings is likely to get you in hot-water very fast with most actors. And rightly so. In comedy, it's a little harder to avoid — especially if the actor isn't finding the rhythm of the line. But hopefully you've cast well and that's not an issue. But… Big but… If you've tried leading the horse to water a few times, and the line just isn't funny — and you know it's funny another way: Don't pretend the actors reading is funny if it's not. Take the actor aside —

PRIVATELY — and say something like this: "Okay. I feel like a total dick here, and I NEVER do this... But, dude, this is a really funny line and we're not hitting the comedy as hard as we can. Can I tell you what word I think needs to be hit. I just have to trust my gut here — for both of us."

Now I want to talk about prepping to actually shoot a scene on the day. I came a bit late to this discipline and I have to credit the great Director of Photography, John Bailey, for beating it into me. Make sure before a single shot is fired off that EVERYONE on your crew knows the scene and knows the blocking. I was, in the beginning, constantly 'rushing' and skipping this step. I'd always (almost) rehearse the actors, usually alone. Then I might (usually) have a chat with the DP and tell him what I was generally thinking. But then I'd want to clear the set, so the DP could start lighting and I could shoot. That one or two minutes that it takes to 'run' the scene for the entire crew: Sound (especially), but also props and hair/makeup, script supervisor — I just couldn't get in the habit of doing it. It seemed a waste of time. We had to do a master after all and the crew could see the blocking then. Then along came John Bailey, who was older (a bit), smarter (a lot), and way way tougher than me. He basically told me what an ass I was being for not allowing my collaborators to do their best work. Without seeing the scene rehearsed, they could not make any preparations that they might otherwise have made. Certainly this makes sense for Sound — For starters, because they could be thinking where the boom guy was gonna be, where the boom itself was gonna be. Poor Sound. Alas, the Sound Dept. is almost ALWAYS under-respected on a set. (But fear not: They have the last laugh. Post Production is a fucking nightmare when sound issues haven't been carefully and properly addressed during production.)

How does being prepared or un-prepared for a project affect your abilities as a director? How does preparation change your mind-set? What shifts or changes go on within you?

As said above, when I'm prepared I bring a relaxation to the set that is otherwise hard to summon. I bring focus and I bring vision. I am a vastly better communicator (and collaborator) when I've done the things I've listed above. Do I always do them? Nope. I don't. And occasionally (rarely) it turns out very well. Mostly, it doesn't turn out well. It just 'gets done'. The more prep I do, the more I'm able to participate in the aliveness of the set.

Sleep, by the way, counts as preparation. As does eating. Most of us can function without enough sleep. But there is a big difference between functioning and doing the gig right. My crews usually laughs at me, but I don't think I've missed a 15-30 minute nap one day of production. It's how I spend lunch — then grab a light meal after I wake. I can't be present or alert — and my capacity to see and hear — all take a plunge when I'm fatigued.

As for food, directing with wheat in my body is like swimming through drying cement. It's my only fixed and rigid no-no. I'm a thousand percent Gluten Free. But that's just me.

Do you have a pre-shoot ritual? If so, what is it?

I always make sure I have a great pair of glasses before

I start a film. Or a few pairs. It's funny. My first film I had three pairs hanging off different necklaces. One for distance. One for reading. One for the monitor. And there was probably a pair of sunglasses in a pocket too. Finally, on my third flick I got transitional progressive lenses. All-In-One. Wow.. Night and day. No going back.

I also try to make sure I'm as fit as possible. I'll usually lose 5-10 pounds. I'll start to do yoga and/or exercise more readily. Production is brutal. The hours are perverse. It's great to be ready to meet the beast.

Have there ever been times where you did not prepare as best as you could? If so, what happened and what did you learn?

As I've said, there are plenty of times I haven't done my homework. The less I've done, the more stressful the day will be. And above and beyond the anxiety and discomfort of working on the fly, there's the very real chance that you are going to live with the result of this failure to prepare for a long, long time. Anyone who has directed knows the agony of having to put a scene that sucks in your film because the film requires it. It's awful. And it's even more awful if the scene that you will live with forever sucks because you weren't prepared. I endeavor to NEVER put myself in the position — by lack of planning — where I might totally screw up a scene and have to accept it and live with it. There are scenes from old flicks I can't watch. I'll fast-forward (or, as a friend suggested, look at my feet). You only have to do it once to realize it's no fun. If we do the work to prepare for the day, all goes far, far better.

How does your preparation differ in each stage of production? And in turn how is your leadership approach different for development, pre-production, production, and post-production?

I've probably touched on it elsewhere, but I should mention that the further into production I get, the more deeply I am collaborating and co-creating. In the beginning, I'm far more 'authoritative', in the sense that I am the authority. I'm the one who has either written the script, or has at least come to a very deep understanding of it. And so, at the outset, I'm usually the one setting the table for others. But fairly quickly — especially if, like my actors, I've chosen my crew well — those men and women are starting to develop their own (almost always great) ideas. Some directors bristle a bit at this. But not me. I long for the collaboration. The sum of our visions — as long as we are all springing from a single and clear premise or idea — is usually better.

That said, it must ALWAYS come down to the director. I became a far better director when I stopped needing everyone to admire, respect or even like me. This, above all, is probably the best prep you can do: Grow up. Toss out Narcism and its cousin self-loathing. Find a place within yourself where you're 'enough'. Cultivate it and guard it. Figure out what makes you 'enough'. And be fucking enough.

When I'm in that space there is a TON of room for you, there is a TON of room for any good idea that comes my way. When I'm NOT enough, then there is far less room, because I'm operating under the excruciating misconception that my performance as a director is somehow required to finally make me feel loved. If you don't know what I'm talking about, you're lucky. If you do, and you haven't done so already, try directing without the horrible bonds of needing to prove fucking anything. Just do your best. Be kind — at all times. Be understanding. Tell the truth. And endeavor to get truth on the screen. That's what they're coming for.

What are some resources or strategies you would suggest aspiring directors use for preparing for a shoot?

Pushups. Hikes. Yoga. Therapy if needed.

Any other comments or stories that you would like to add?

To any offended by such things, forgive my brief dip into spirituality for a moment. But I find the Serenity Prayer is very very helpful as a director:

God — and AA is very kind about allowing multiple interpretations of this idea called God — *grant me Serenity to Accept the things I cannot change; Courage to Change the things I can. And Wisdom to know the difference.*

It's that last part — Wisdom — that will make a huge difference before, during and after production. It is imperative that we pick our fights; that we recognize which ones we can win — and/or should win. And which ones aren't going to go our way. If that's the case, if we need to accept something that's not going to go the way we'd like, the earlier we realize this the better.

And as the first two bits of the prayer suggest, once you've figured out which column the thing belongs in, you can do the sometimes harder work of Accepting or Courageously Changing. But the Wisdom comes first. Or should. That said, I've probably figured out the hard way whether I was supposed to accept or change more times than I can count. Wisdom, like magic hour, is finite.

3

COMMAND THE ROOM

HAVE YOU EVER BEEN to an event or party and someone entered the room and everyone looked at him or her? Have you ever thought about why that is? Is it because everyone knows who they are? Is it because they are smart? Is it because they are beautiful? Or maybe it's because of how they carry themselves when they walk in.

There are a handful of people that I have met over the years who have the unique ability to command a room. All of them hold a few things in common. For one, they are all confident in who they are and their abilities. They all dress well and take good care of themselves physically. In my observations of myself and others it comes down to confidence. To command a room, you have to be 100% confident because people will see that on your face and in your body language.

There have been times when I've arrived on set completely exhausted, but I didn't let that affect my confidence because at the end of the day I had a job to do and I had to make sure that it got done. In July of 2014, I had the finale shoot for the second season of *Out Of Frame,* an edutainment web series that I produce. I had just come back from Punta Cana the day before. I had done most of the prep work before I left for my trip, but I knew there would be a handful of tasks to complete the day I got back. I unfortunately had so much to do that I only got about an hour and a half of sleep the day before the biggest and most complex shoot of the season. No matter though! I woke up at 6:00am because I had to pack the truck with everything. I arrived on set feeling quite tired but once the crew arrived, I forgot about the fact that I had barely had any sleep and I jumped right into the action. Since the shoot was a bit nuts and we were really strapped for time, I had to command the room to make sure that we stayed focused and on schedule.

> "Directing is really exciting. In the end, it's more fun to be the painter than the paint."
> - George Clooney

When all eyes and ears are on you, it's a bit odd at first, but it is a nice confidence booster. When you're addressing actors or the group, people are looking to you for direction. You're the voice of reason. If you are in command of the room, then when you say "That's a wrap!", it means that it's a wrap.

All of this is not to say that you should be Mr. or Mrs. Bossypants the second you step through the door. It's quite the opposite actually. Commanding the room with positive energy and enthusiasm is the way right way to do it. People respond very quickly to energy. So it's no wonder that a bad day on set may have started with some Negative Ned or Nancy coming into the studio feeling sad and telling everyone about it.

You can choose to command the room in a way that motivates and inspires the people around you, or you can lay on the guilt, or you can choose to command the room like a dictator. You do have the choice so it is up to you to make the responsible decision. Of course, there are times when you'll have woken up on the wrong side of the bed and you may snap. In that scenario it would be your recovery of the situation that defines who you are as a director.

The role of a director is exhausting and can take its toll on a person's physical state and emotions. Exhaustion can have an effect on one's ability to lead properly. A good leader will be aware of his or her own mental and physical state and be able to manage it wisely so that it doesn't affect his or her ability to direct.

It takes a lot of assertiveness and self-awareness to command a room for many long days which can become draining. Going back to the very first chapter, know thyself. You need to know what your breaking points are and take note of moments when your fuse is shortening. If you've been commanding a room with your amazing leadership for 10 hours and there's two hours to go in the day and you can feel yourself spiralling downward then take a break, regroup, and return with a clear head. Leadership isn't about telling others what to do – anyone can do that. Leadership is about being in control of yourself and being fully aware of the things and people around you. A great leader can change the way he or she commands a room and can shift the energy of a group naturally.

The ability to command the room doesn't always come naturally to people though. Sometimes it requires one to do or say certain things to muster up the level of confidence needed to truly command a room, since at the end of the day it really is about having a high level of self-confidence. People are attracted to other people with confidence. If you walk into the room with poise and conviction to accomplish your goals people will respect you. I do that naturally when I'm in an environment that I'm comfortable in, like being on set or in the post-production edit suites. There are days when I may be less confident and slightly nervous because I'm attempting to do something I haven't done before. One example of this was when I had to block out a critical comedic stunt for the *Out Of Frame* episode about The Marx Brothers. I'm not a stunt coordinator, but since I didn't have the budget to hire one, I had to figure out a safe but effective way of doing the stunt. Thankfully the actor performing it had some previous stunt training so the move looked hilarious and real on camera.

There are some days you have to improvise and it won't always work out. It's those days when I need a pick-me-up or a bit of extra motivation. Every director will have one of those days at some point. It is helpful to do some additional preparation before arriving on set which may mean wearing a certain item of clothing, eating a certain kind of food, or saying certain affirmations to yourself.

– BONUS –

For a complete list of positive affirmations please visit:
beyondthedirectorschair.com/bookbonus
and download the PDF.

On days when I'm a bit nervous (and even on days when I'm just excited) I like to do two things. First I relax and get in the zone, then I tell myself that the day is going to go smoothly. I clear my head, take some deep breaths and confirm aloud all the things I want to accomplish. After I do that I feel much more confident and ready to be an effective leader.

I also find that giving myself affirmations throughout the day helps me keep positive, but I have to give most of the credit of my sanity on set to the people I work with. They are the people who keep me motivated and smiling all day long. Shoots can get quite stressful, especially on shoots where I act as producer as well as director.

I can't recall a time when I've had a bad experience when arriving on set. I do remember one time when I was in school and I was shooting a video short for a class project. It was my turn to direct since it was my story and at first it was great, but as the day went on I struggled to keep control of the set. It became a challenge because there were a couple of people on set giving me some push back and not listening to my direction. I was being very serious and they were being silly which is why I felt like I was losing control and not commanding the room. I was so serious because I felt pressure to do well on the project since I had to keep my grades up to keep a scholarship. Since I had good relationships with the people I was working with luckily there was no animosity on set despite the miscommunications. If I could go back I would have been much less serious and I'm quite certain that it would have solved all the issues that I was having on set that day.

In high school I had a couple of experiences directing school plays. In both cases I worked with co-directors. It is in these situations when every director wants to command the room and creative clashes occur. There were a few bumps along the way during rehearsals, but in the end we got what we wanted from the performers and everyone involved had a great time. It's important to understand that commanding a room does not mean that the person doing so must have the biggest ego. In fact, it's quite the opposite. When a director truly commands the room he or she has self-confidence and humbleness at the same time. Having high self-confidence tells the people you work with that you can make decisions and handle whatever outcomes may occur. Great directors can admit they are wrong without embarrassment and can take full responsibility for the results, even if others had a part in what happened. It takes a person with unbounded self-confidence and a very high level of ethics to do that.

Aside from figuring out the vision for a project, figuring out the shots and blocking, and guiding the performances, a director's job is to lead and manage a team to successfully tell a stunning visual story. Be the director that people want to look up to and the person that people are inspired by. Be the director that works twice as hard as everyone else to show that you are grateful for the opportunity you've been given. The moment when you decide that you are that director, you've given yourself all the confidence you need to command a room.

There is also the other side of that coin. It isn't uncommon to hear stories about directors with bad reputations. Most of the time it has nothing to do with whether the person is good or bad at their core because most people are good, it is simply about how they choose to carry themselves and behave on set.

So how does one avoid a bad reputation? In my opinion the answer is simple: be an effective leader who promotes positivity and acknowledges improvement. Having the power to lead a group doesn't give you the right to use that power to undermine or disrespect others. A director who has a bad reputation may bring about the end result in creating a completed picture, but it doesn't make them a great director. If you think about it they wouldn't really be leading the crew to success, they'd be leading them down a path of fear and constant doubt. Even if a film makes a ton of money in the end, you'll have an entire crew of people who will never want to work with you again.

To me, no amount of money or success can replace the respect you get from hard working crew and dedicated actors. The concept is clear - if you treat people well and give them acknowledgement and praise when they do good work then they will be more productive because they will want to work harder. Do that, and you'll always get a completed film or series that everyone is proud of.

> "A director makes 100 decisions an hour. Students ask me how you know how to make the right decision, and I say to them, 'If you don't know how to make the right decision, you're not a director."
> **- George Lucas**

When I command a room I do it with respect for everyone else in the room and I recognize the skills that they bring to the table.

TIPS AND TRICKS

Three things you can say or do to command a room are:

1. Enter smiling and leave laughing.

2. Stand tall and proud. The job you are doing isn't easy so take pride that you're actually pulling it off.

3. Speak clearly and confidently. Enunciate your words.

These three simple steps sound nice, but they only become easy by turning them into habits. Make a conscious effort to do these on every project you direct.

A trick you can use if you're a tad bit nervous is to stand with your hands on your hips and with your head held high, like a superhero stance, for several minutes before entering the room. Doing that boosts your testosterone levels and in turn you feel more confident. I've used this technique a multitude of times when I've been nervous and it works like a charm every time.

Here are some other suggestions to make taking control of the room feel a bit less overwhelming:

1. Use your hands. I talk with my hands without thinking about it, but if you're more reserved then using your hands and arms while you talk can help get everyone's attention. Too much motion can make people dizzy though, so just be aware.

2. If you find that you're commanding a room but people are interpreting it as bossy and don't respond

to you the way you'd like then maybe you need to shift your approach. Say what you want to have happen then follow it up by simply asking your key crew if they have any suggestions on making it happen. Asking others for their input makes them feel included even if you don't use their ideas.

3. Volume Control. It's a term most of us know from childhood but it's one we can forget in high speed and high intensity environments. Be aware of your volume. Only raise your voice when it's absolutely necessary, and even then, try to avoid it. Nobody wants to be yelled at even if it is unintentional. Your self-awareness and your awareness of the situation in front of you should dictate your volume. Ideally you should reserve the yelling only for when you say 'action' or 'cut'.

Commanding a room is really about being able to hold your own and be confident enough to not give your power away to others. Your power doesn't refer to the control you have over others, it refers to your own self-governance and dignity. Own the fact that you are in a position of influence as a director, just don't abuse it. There is a fine line between being the boss and being bossy.

INTERVIEW WITH
GAIL HARVEY

Murdoch Mysteries, Lost Girl, Heartland, Some Things That Stay, Rickie Lee Jones: The Other Side of Desire

Why do you think it's important for a director to command the room?

It is very important for a director to command the room because it gives everyone confidence that you can do your job and do it well. There is nothing worse than a director that appears unsure and indecisive. Sometimes crews smell blood - but it is usually because they are working on a TV show for many seasons and they are worried you will ruin their show. Or on a feature film set they will be worried it will be a bad experience. Everyone's job is harder when there is no leader.

What has been the best or worst experience when it comes to your arrival on set and 'commanding the room'?

I am a very confident person and also I am a nice person. I don't believe in yelling or making life difficult for people. I believe everyone is on a set to do the best job they can do and it is my job to make the set a place where people feel they can do their best work and also contribute, be heard, but the decisions are up to me. Dan Petrie Sr. was a mentor of mine and he used to say "Gail, a film set is a very collaborative place, but it must never be a democracy."

Probably my best experience was when the crew applauded because I had arrived. Probably my worst experience was when I was the third female director on a TV show, and when I arrived the director of photography said "Oh no, not another woman director......." I'm happy to say the show I directed was a huge success!

What do you say to yourself before heading to set?

Before I head to set I make sure I do my homework and have a game plan. I do a shot list and figure out blocking and camera positions, etc, but then never look a them. The prep you do beforehand allows you to work instinctively.

Do affirmations or self-talk help you with your job?

I don't really do self-talk or affirmations, but I do meditate and I do yoga — often on set I do yoga breathing — I find remaining calm is a very good thing on set and in life.

What would you suggest to up-and-coming directors to ensure that they maintain a professional reputation in the industry? How can they make sure to not cross the line when it comes to commanding the room?

Remember filmmaking is a collaborative art form – whether on TV or film sets. Trust your actors to bring their life to your set and to do a great job. Have a plan, but listen to your director of photography – he might have a better plan. There is a fine line between being in charge and collaborative, and being in charge but limiting the creativity on a set because you feel you have to be in control.

The role of a director can be very exhausting and can take its tole on a person's physical state and his or her emotions. In turn, this can have an effect on the ability to lead properly. What do you feel is the best strategy when it comes to dealing with exhaustion while still holding command of the room?

Yes, it is a very gruelling job - physically and mentally. I try to be prepared and organized so I rarely do overtime (I feel a twelve hour day is enough!!!) I also eat well, exercise and try to handle the day to day stresses in a strong but classy way. If there is a problem with someone I never speak to them in front of people. I take them aside and speak calmly. When I am directing actors I go to them and talk in a quiet way and I don't talk too much, but communicate honestly.

Any other comments or stories that you would like to add?

I just want to say that I feel I have the best job in the world, and I love being on set. It is an amazing thing to move the boulder up the hill with all your cast and crew working together to make the best work possible.

4

EXUDE POSITIVE ENERGY

THIS SOUNDS A LOT simpler than it is for many people. Directing anything requires a huge amount of focus, work ethic, and enthusiasm. You may have moments when the stress of the job affects how positive you are around other people. It would be prudent to be highly aware of your attitude and mind-set because people will feed off your energy, whether you are aware of it or not and whether you like it or not. To exude positive energy successfully you have to leave any stress or worry you have in your personal life at home because having those negative emotions has an effect on your ability to see things clearly. And frankly, since you will be putting out fire after fire and making non-stop decisions, you won't even have time to think about your own problems.

At the beginning of the shoot I always like to have a team meeting to make sure everyone is working towards the same purpose. Even if I am tired, I make sure to have high energy right off the bat so that it spreads to the rest of the team. By making sure I have high energy it helps the day go smoothly because I have noticed that people are more productive and efficient when their energy levels are high and when they have a positive and fun approach to things.

Having a positive attitude on set makes a difference whether it is a small shoot with less than ten crew members or a big blockbuster film with over two hundred crew members. It's amazing how much one's attitude towards working affects their productivity and happiness. People like being productive and feeling good about their work. I know because I've not only been there but I've seen it. The times when my cast and crew had high energy are the times where they tend to be more efficient in getting tasks done and are also more aware of the things happening around them. When problems arise they are solved much more quickly when people have positive attitudes and high energy.

There was one time on set when the boom operator was helping the grip assistant with changing a lightbulb and the lightbulb broke. He cut his finger and we were down one light but the day continued with no problems. I only found out about it later on because instead of panicking and making a big deal about it, the boom operator and some of the other crew handled the problem with no fuss and moved on. Had their attitudes been crappy I can guarantee that situation would have gone a totally different way.

> "I wouldn't take a directing job if I didn't think it was enriching life."
> - Baz Luhrmann

I make sure that I am consciously smiling and laughing on set. Whether people look to me as a leader or not, I have to be one. If I start to dwindle as the director and/or producer then the rest of the crew gets dragged down with me even if it isn't intentional. Sometimes people don't realize it's even happening so you have to be hyper conscious of how you are behaving so that you can stay in control of the energy you put out on set. I learned this the hard way. The moment that I started to change my attitude everything around me began to shift. It seems so simple, but it takes self-awareness and openness to change your behaviour to actually see the results.

I have had my moments of frustration on set and have been 100% aware of them, but I've made the mistake of not handling it right away. Of course this slows down the set and makes it extra difficult to recover from. The worst part of what happens if my attitude goes south is that not only are people less motivated, but it completely stunts the productivity of everyone on set. As a director you want a set that is moving efficiently and a set on which everyone is having a great time. This is especially crucial on big budget sets where an extra hour of shooting could mean tens of thousands of dollars. A positive attitude from the leader is the source of great results.

Since I've become quite aware of negative attitudes and energies it becomes apparent to me very quickly when there is a negative force on set pulling things down. On a small set it is easy to spot where it is originating from but it can sometimes be a challenge on a larger set because often times it is more than one person. I have been lucky enough to have worked with people who are amazing and who are a joy to have around. There have been slip ups and small incidences where a performer gets frustrated or when a crew member is having an off-day and the way to handle that is easy.

You simply pull them aside at an appropriate time and ask them if everything is alright. Tell them that you noticed they seem a bit off and that it is having an effect on the rest of the crew. Sometimes people are totally unaware that their negativity is contagious, just as positive energy is. Make them aware of it and that should completely solve the problem because they'll be much more conscious of their behaviour for the rest of the day, and for the remainder of the production schedule. Of course if the issue continues then it becomes a deeper discussion where you may have to refer to the code of conduct and policies. Most of the time there isn't a clause in the contract they signed off on about behaviour unless it is unlawful and/or violent so it is not useful to use that in a meeting. It can help to ask them what their career goals are and remind them that this project is a part of building their career. Their attitude on one shoot can determine how others remember them, and the same truth applies to you as the director.

Having positive energy and an enthusiastic attitude is important in any aspect of production because it keeps things going and produces better results across the board (better performances, better productivity, and even better box office numbers).

There were moments on the set of *Out Of Frame* when I would get frustrated because there were certain things that pushed us back and forced us to improvise on the spot. I rarely let it get to the point where I was losing my cool, but I know that the crew and cast could see that I was frustrated.

Exude Positive Energy

We would push through the frustration because there was nothing else we could do. The nature of low budget independent productions is that there will usually be some sort of challenge that comes up. For us it tended to be audio related. We were filming in studios that were not properly soundproofed (because we were working off a small budget) so we would have to work around the noises above and around us. Since we had to continuously retake scenes because noises would pop up in the middle of a line, I had to make sure that I was not being super picky with the delivery of lines. In those moments I had to mute my inner perfectionist and stay efficient to ensure that I got everything I needed.

In those moments of frustration it is my crew that brings me back down to earth. Laughing it off makes it much easier to handle those kinds of tense situations. I also find it helpful to have another producer on set who is disciplined and who has an amazing positive attitude. That way when I am focused on directing the other producer can keep track of how we are doing for time and if there does happen to be an issue that arises then the producer can help with controlling the situation.

When I am directing for a client video I always have positive energy and if an issue comes up then I don't let the client know about it. I just handle it. The most unprofessional thing to do would be to have a client see the problems that are happening when they are paying you for your skills. It is great leadership practice for directors to do commercial gigs because it allows you to be in control under a different kind of pressure.

My suggestion for a director who is just starting out would be to start out on a smaller commercial or independent production sets because those will be the best environments in which to practice your leadership skills since larger scale projects are different environments with bigger challenges and more people to manage.

Once I arrived early to the location we had booked for a shoot. It was freezing outside and all the crew and I wanted in that moment was to be indoors. I sprawled myself against the front door of the location and made some silly faces and motions whilst fake yelling "let us in!". It seemed to entertain a few of the crew members and lightened the mood since we were all wet and cold. It also allowed me to start my day off on a high note.

I try to be silly as much as I can especially on set because it gets people smiling and laughing and it sets the tone for the shoot. One thing to note is that you can't fake positive energy. People will see right through that and will have little to no reason to like or respect you. Your attitude and behaviour has to be genuine in order to have the desired effect on others.

I can't remember a time on the set of *Out Of Frame* where I wasn't giggling, though most often it was under my breath while the cameras were rolling so as to not screw up a shot. It always helps to have performers who don't take themselves too seriously and who know how to laugh at themselves.

Even in post-production, have a silly disposition while sitting with the editor in the edit suite. Editing requires one to be hyper-focused for long hours, so do your best to create a fun atmosphere. I sometimes like posting funny videos or photos on social media.

Laughter keeps the room light. One of your main priorities should be making sure that everyone is enjoying themselves, so you need to find ways to make that happen without it wasting time or detracting from getting work done. If something hilarious happens, take the moment to acknowledge it and laugh about it with your colleagues.

In what is often a high pressure environment on a set, finding moments to lighten the mood helps keep the crew and cast level-headed. It can be more of a challenge to do this on a project where the plot of the story or the themes are more serious or controversial, but still make an effort to find an appropriate time to be silly.

> "A film is - or should be - more like music than like fiction. It should be a progression of moods and feelings. The theme, what's behind the emotion, the meaning, all that comes later."
> **- Stanley Kubrick**

To give an example of that, I directed a short film called *A Last Wish*, which is about a 70 year old woman named Shayna who must decide whether to grant her father's wish to die with dignity. While filming a story like that which explores a more controversial topic like physician assisted suicide, there were seldom parts in the script that were silly or funny. So I did my best to find times in between takes to share a good chuckle with my wonderful cast and crew about something unrelated to the actual story. We had a scene that took place in a palliative care facility (though we shot it in a private hospital) where the lead characters were talking and walking down a hallway, and one of the extras was in a wheelchair and had to be pushed down the hall in the background by another extra playing a nurse. Between each take the background performers would trade places, and with a running start would push the wheelchair back to the first mark. Someone filmed the two actors having so much fun speeding down the hall in this wheelchair, and the video became a source of entertainment throughout the day.

Exuding positive energy doesn't necessarily mean that you always have to be smiling from ear to ear. It can mean that you are conscious of the tone of the room and behave accordingly. You want everyone to be in a working environment that they can leave at the end of the day with a smile on their face. If people are going home at the end of a long shoot day with scowls on their faces, you know that you aren't doing the best job of oozing positive energy.

It is understandable that sometimes the stress of directing can get to you, but just remember, to quote Bob Marley, "don't worry, be happy". Having a positive attitude can bolster the breathtaking moments and uplift the frustrating ones.

You have a job that many people would love to have so don't tarnish the amazing gift you've been given by walking around with a stick up your butt. When you first start out and it's tough to find paid directing gigs, it might feel like you're trying to push a boulder up a huge mountain, but it's a positive attitude that will get you through any struggle. Treat people well and exude happiness because that's what your cast and crew will remember you for.

INTERVIEW WITH
STEFAN BROGREN

Degrassi: The Next Generation, Open Heart,
The L.A. Complex

Why did you choose this chapter?

Nothing shuts down a set quicker than a feeling of sorrow. I think that it's very easy for a set to feel mundane and lose its energy and feel like it's a job, and lose that that creative force to move forward with everyone. Your crew really wants to be able to enjoy their jobs, they got into the film industry for a reason so they want to make sure that their day is challenging and rewarding as well. I've seen it when sets just lose that that enthusiasm, and it can kill a day.

It's definitely a trickle down effect and it does come from the top a little bit, from the producers, directors, and the writers. I think sometimes people start to second guess themselves when they're in a situation where they're not getting, it doesn't even have to be a positive attitude, but a clear and defined vision.

Negativity can be taken as sort of like uncertainty. When that happens it trickles down and people start to second guess, whether it be your camera ops and so forth all the way to the actors. It's one of those things that causes a whole crew to end up feeling lost. By a positive attitude, we're not talking about play time, but we're definitely talking about keeping the energy up and keeping people involved.

I'm a big one to ask most departments what they think of the scene just to keep them involved. I don't know how often they get asked what they thought of a scene, but it does keep them feeling a little bit more like they're a part of the process, and that changes everything. This is an industry that can in real life be a very monotonous job, and maybe not creatively rewarding. I like to think that if they feel like they're involved then that just improves the product altogether.

I've dealt with negativity on set in a positive way and in a negative way. I'm speaking from experience where I know I've been unsatisfied with a scene and if I've expressed that too visibly then that could be something that crosses the board with everyone else, and then everyone starts to ask 'what are we doing?'.

I remember when I was shooting webisodes for *Degrassi* and we were doing a Hallowe'en special and it was supposed to be sort of based on *Carrie*. A bunch of blood had to be thrown on a bunch of kids. It was a big bucket of red paint and it missed the mark and it didn't hit the actors where it was supposed to. I kind of had a little bit of a flip out because I didn't have the time or money to reset. It was a one shot deal.

I don't even remember being upset. The people recall how upset I was, and it really put a damper on the speed and accuracy for the rest of the day. So I knew I should never let that happen again.

That was one of those things where where my negative attitude definitely trickled down. I remember one of my very good friends who is a producer on the show saying you know that 'We gotta turn this around, you gotta really sort of forget this and move on'. I didn't even realize that I was negative. It is something you have to be conscious of.

I've been in situations with people when there might be confusion from any number of departments and I've had to just figure that out in my head without actually causing any panic, because at that point it becomes, well, if the director doesn't know what he's doing then we're in real trouble.

Just going a little bit zen sometimes and allowing yourself to look past the minutia that's around you, whether it be an actor who doesn't like his blocking or the writers who are going 'You have to hit this beat, you haven't hit it' - and suddenly you're just like 'Oh, that's going to put me a couple of hours behind'. How do you fix that without actually flipping out and just truck forward?

It sounds kind of crazy just to 'think positive', but it actually makes a huge difference. I've relied on it so much, especially on a show like *Degrassi* where we don't do overtime. We have a very strict 11 hour day and so if we don't make our day, we don't make our day. I rely on that crew to be on my side and pushing forward, so a positive attitude has to happen.

How do you demonstrate a positive attitude on set? Explain what you consciously say and/or do.

I don't know, maybe it's in my personality. I talk a lot and I might over talk as far as what my intentions of a scene are even if it's a very simple one. That can be confusing. You do have to edit yourself sometimes because too much information can lead an actor or your DP in the wrong direction.

I find that having good conversation with the actors on the floor and finding the fun, even if it's a horrific scene, really helps. Trying to find a little bit of levity before you get into shooting something really heavy helps.

I find that behind the camera the conversation can't stop. There are those directors who are very stoic and like to stay to themselves. That can be a thing where you're just leaving people in the lurch, where they're wondering if the director is enjoying it, if he likes what's happening, or if it's a failure. You'll talk to the director later and they'll think everything's going great. You have to pass that information on. It's something that I find really useful.

What have you noticed in terms of the way people behave or work differently because of your positive energy? How does that impact the end result?

You know it's funny because I was talking to an actor the other day who I worked with years ago who was saying 'Do you remember when you had to call me over and tell me I wasn't pulling my weight?' I think I was asked to do that by one of the producers and I was like dreading it because you never want to be the bad cop.

I found myself trying to find a way of doing that that didn't seem totally humiliating to the guy, because I don't think he recognized that he wasn't pulling his weight. I had to pull him aside, which is already a bad feeling you know.

It's not a good thing when someone goes 'Can I talk to you for a minute?'. I gently said 'I'm not going to be the first one to tell you this, but several of the producers are going to be telling you'. I totally passed the buck in a lot of ways, but I made it very clear that we had to change whatever his attitude was right away. He said that it was a major turning point for him. I know that the rest of the day he kicked ass. So sometimes it's telling someone in a way that's sensitive, but it's also about reminding them how great the project is. Why would you want to jeopardize that?

For me what happens is if I go silent people are really surprised and then they are wondering what's going on because I am pretty chatty when I'm working. They're thinking I might be dissatisfied with what's happening on set or that there might be confusion, or wonder if I really have my plan together.

I like a loud set, I mean I don't like it when we're two hours behind, but I do like people to feel like it's active. You can tell when the place has gone silent. People are doing their jobs but they're just going through the motions.

It's infectious when you are passing along your attitude to others. If I didn't actually have a plan when I was on set then everyone would know. If we're trucking along and people really don't know what my vision is, then we all feel lost and people wonder why they're doing it.

Why do you think having a positive energy is important?

When I'm in pre-production, which is by far the most boring part of the whole process, I'm trying to figure out what I have at my disposal. Can I actually get that special lens? How I am supposed to shoot twelve pages in a day? Realizing that you can't shoot a certain scene because it just doesn't work into your schedule. That's the time where you can easily drift off and become passive. I know that I've done it and in the first steps of pre-production that can be death.

By keeping conversations going and talking about the minutia of something then at least you have all of your bases covered, so that when you're going through it, everyone is active. You can be in a production meeting and see people with their eyes totally closed, like completely sleeping. You try to make sure that those people are part of the conversation because when you're on the floor you don't want them missing that stuff that was supposed to be there.

The people I work with are fantastic, I don't want to say that anyone really screws up or anything like that, but there are those times when people sort of start to drift off and lose interest in a product. For us to keep our energy up and have a positive attitude really makes the difference between a set that is prepared and a set that feels lost.

It's hard to fake also. Hopefully you're involved in a project you actually are excited about. It must be hard when you have to do industrials. If you're starting out as a director and you're doing industrials for companies, how do you keep motivated and think that you're doing something that's important and creatively satisfying? So it might be tough in those situations.

I've been very lucky to have things that I really care about. I love the creative, that's where the fun is and where you find more than what was on the page.

What piece of advice would you give an aspiring director (in relation to being positive)?

When I was just starting out my buddies and I were all completely broke and not having a clue of how to get into the industry. We just didn't know how to do it. I was an actor, so how do you transition from being an actor to something that's behind the camera and get taken seriously?

Those little crappy projects that you have to do along the way and creating your own content obviously can feel like an uphill battle that doesn't seem to have any end in sight. You don't realize what a big difference the little steps you're taking are making.

Me and my buddy, Samir Rehem, who has also directed on *Degrassi*, did this film when we were 27 years old for like $80,000 bucks and we shot it in a day. It was a concept thing where we actually wanted to do a house party. Mini DV tapes just came out and thought that we could totally shoot a movie in one day. We hired twelve actors and we had them improv inside an actual party that we were throwing with like two hundred people. It was mayhem. It was a mixture of our friends and twelve actors going through their personal story as they were moving through the party. We thought we were geniuses!

That was one of those things where we were very motivated to finish and then we didn't get into a single festival, we couldn't get anywhere, but then we made two sales. We sold to IFC and to The Movie Network.

I think we actually made our money back, but it wasn't one of those things where we were rolling in it by any means. The planning that went into it was easily eight months to try to get this thing together and I don't think at the time we recognized what it had done. So many people hired us based on that film. Actors who I know got hired out of it as well.

It's one of those things where you have to push forward. You want something substantial and fantastic to come out of that little project right away and it never happens that way 90% of the time.

We had to look at those little steps that happened in between and how everything affected where we are today. It made such a difference. It's just not happening over night. You have to be weary of the fear that you're not going to have that success and just keep trucking forward.

If you have the creative spunk, for lack of a better word, to keep moving forward and the drive, in the end it can be a super fantastic career you didn't even know was happening.

Romona Barckert, this amazing writer who writes on *Degrassi*, and I did this series called *Open Heart* and we were talking about it when she was just coming up the ranks. A day didn't go by, and still doesn't, where she didn't sit at her computer and write something. She feels that if she stops then everything stops, her career stops. That work ethic and that forcing forward definitely put her where she is today.

That feeling of like 'I have to do something creative today to just try to keep the juices flowing'. You might say 'Oh my god, I can't believe I made that piece of crap way back when', but you were doing something that day.

Samir and I would make these terrible shorts when we were in our twenties and we would show them at comedy nights at bars just because we had time on our hands. I was an unemployed actor, he was an editor and we would just try to make anything we could, just for our own benefit. People come up to us today that are in the industry and say they remember them. It's another thing that can start a conversation that leads to a job or another creative opportunity.

Don't take for granted the time you have off. It's important to take advantage of that.

When you go out with friends who are in the industry, the conversations always turn to these subjects because you're constantly trying to push forward. It's a career like any other and you're always thinking what the next step might be.

Sometimes that inner voice just wants to tell you to stop fighting. Your mind melts when you think about how often you have to push through your inner voice telling you it isn't going to happen.

Any other comments or stories that you would like to add?

You know it's funny...everything I've said to you, it's all really just a theory you know because when you get on the floor, you don't know what's going to happen, and all hell can break lose and that positive energy that we were talking about can easily go away.

I don't know if you know, but *Degrassi* got cancelled and got picked up by Netflix within a matter of about a month and a half. For a month and a half I didn't have a job and for the first time in a long time had to think about applying to other companies for other jobs. I was freaking out. If I had six months to know about it I would have lined myself up for another thing, but at that point the summer was gone. So in the meantime I was writing all these ridiculous things just for myself, and one of those things is now in development because of the time I had off going through my crazy period. It's the time that you're at your lowest or at a time where you're feeling like there's nothing lined up where great things happen.

I mean watching Linda and Steven (with DHX, who owns Epitome Pictures, that does *Degrassi*) do this transition over to Netflix was the most exciting thing that happened in their careers. We were fourteen years into a series and now we're actually rebirthing it. Talk about having creative excitement. We sat down and we went 'How are we making *Degrassi* new?' – from the writers, to how we shoot it, to how I'm directing it. How do you open an episode on Netflix where people are binge watching it? You want to make sure that they know a new episode has started because when one starts in the corner fifteen seconds later and you're not watching, you're like 'Wait, did a new episode start?' We had to rethink those things and that is so much fun. Talk about having a positive attitude right now, everyone is just sort of revitalized. I deal with a lot of crew members that I've dealt with for about ten years and to see them get excited about something is very cool. It really has been a real great opportunity for us.

I love working on the show. There can be those days where you might say 'Ugh, this is monotonous, it's been so long in this one world'. And then you kind of go 'Am I kidding myself? This is the best job ever!' You gotta find what you loved about it in the first place so that you realize that you're so lucky.

When I talk to crew members they're so proud when they tell their friends and family because everyone knows *Degrassi*. The show is the best school ever (for actors). I've seen so many people come in that were decent young actors and leave so on top of their game that they've got such a heads up above their competition.

5

BE RESPONSIBLE

TO BE RESPONSIBLE CAN mean a lot of things. Most people would define it as being accountable for someone or something. Others would say that it involves completing important tasks, requires one to make decisions, and to have control. My way of looking at responsibility goes a bit deeper than that. To me responsibility is at the core of everything I do. If I lack responsibility in any area of my life, it has caused me to be fearful to take action and as a result I make mistakes. While making mistakes can be a positive thing most of the time as they bring about learning, making mistakes due to a lack of responsibility can have lasting negative effects.

If you are responsible then you are going into something knowing and accepting any and all of the consequences, and are willing to continue no matter the outcome. So many things can go wrong during a production, but it is the responsibility of the director to deal with the issues and act quickly to implement a solution.

For a director, responsibility spans across everything on

the production from working with the actors to bring out their best performances to making sure that the crew are getting along, and from determining the creative vision for the project to ensuring that the technical decisions made on set or in post-production help the vision come to life. A director is also responsible for knowing a little about a lot because even though the job description of a director is quite straight forward, it's important to have an understanding of all aspects of production from cinematography and visual effects to boom operating and foley. As a director you have to be a great leader and a great learner. You don't need to know everything about everything on a production but you need to know enough that you can effectively communicate with every single crew member and department head. And on top of everything you need to come up with the vision and work with the actors. It's a lot, and it's not for everyone, but if you love it enough and enjoy the process, then you can be a successful director.

As a director you also need to be able to have the same sense of responsibility for others' projects as for your own. If a project is your 'baby' it's easy to adopt a higher level of liability or duty for it, though I have seen situations where directors or creators had little regard for the success of their own projects. It comes down to the amount of passion and motivation one has to see a project come to fruition.

I have a strong sense of responsibility on every project I am a part of. I was asked to direct a short film by a screenwriter I had never met before, and it took me all of five minutes to feel just as responsible for the success of that film as

I do for all of my other projects. I do think that since the job of a director is to bring the words on the page to life through a distinct vision that every project a director works on should bring about a higher level of responsibility every time.

If I had to pick one project that gave me the biggest sense of responsibility I would have to say that it would be *Out Of Frame*, not because of the size and scope of the web series, because I have other projects that are of a much larger scope, but because it was the first project I worked on that allowed me to direct and produce. I am so grateful that I worked on the project and stuck to it for as long as I did as all of the hard work paid off. It is now an award-winning edutainment web series with global distribution. Directing and producing *Out Of Frame* forced me to learn how to be patient on set, how to value and respect people's time and efforts even more, and how to truly be a responsible leader.

Saying 'yes' to more projects despite the fact that my schedule is bonkers can be dangerous as I run the risk of spreading myself too thin, but I like being responsible for a lot. I find that every time I do say yes to a project that I feel strongly about, I adapt my schedule and make time for that project all due to the fact that I have a stake in the project's success. As soon as I am accountable for even a small portion of a project's success, my overall responsibility goes up. I become better at time management and problem solving. With that said, taking on multiple projects at the same time is not necessarily the best decision for you. Though by 'doing' more during a production you will take

> "Eighty percent of success is turning up."
> **- Woody Allen**

more responsibility for things, and as you continue doing more your confidence will go up as quickly as your responsibility does.

There may be times when you'll have to take responsibility for something that someone else has done simply because you are the leader on set. Now this doesn't mean that you take the blame, it means that you are willing to accept the consequences. For example, if an actor doesn't show up on time it can throw off your entire day, which costs the production money. It is your job to re-evaluate and make the most of the day despite the fact that things are running behind. It doesn't help you or the success of the production to whine and complain until the actor shows up and it definitely doesn't help to yell at them when they do show up. A conversation will have to happen between the director or producer and the actor about the importance of being on time, and consequences will have to be agreed upon if it happens again. This is important because as a leader you need to help others understand the consequences of their behaviour.

I've been lucky and haven't yet experienced anything extreme where I've had to take responsibility for something that someone else has done. Of course there are times when people have showed up late, but it's never been so late that I have to change my plan for the production. Those kinds of situations can be avoided by hiring the right people for the job, and this goes for cast or crew. Mistakes made in the hiring phase can have a much bigger impact later on. I have a select group of people that I've worked with over the years and with whom I would work again in a heartbeat because I saw how responsible they were on set.

I do know that if something were to ever happen where I would have to deal with someone else's wrongdoing whether it be small or detrimental to the production there are some key steps that I would follow.

1. **Identify exactly what has been said or done.** None of this "I heard it through the grapevine" nonsense. You should hear it from the horse's mouth.

2. **Determine what the immediate effects are.** Is it something that will require you to change your schedule for the day, or fire someone? Or is it something too minute to have any major effect on the production and can be dealt with at a later time? Figure out what has to be handled right away.

3. **Decide on an action plan.** Make a quick decision about how to handle the situation. The quicker you make your decision, the better. The key with this kind of decision-making is to not let your emotions play into your decision. It's best to make a decision based on facts and truth, otherwise you'll regret it later.

4. **Implement your decision.** Once you have made a decision on how to handle the situation, implement it right away otherwise you run the risk of making the problem grow. Lingering problems get bigger if you do nothing about them. By implementing your decision you are automatically taking responsibility for your decision.

5. **Deal with the consequences of your decision.** Your decision may create positive results or negative results. Either way you have to confront the consequences and deal with them. You want the situation to be at its most ideal state, meaning a state that you can live with comfortably. Any issue needs to have a completed outcome. In other words, there can't be any part of the problem that is unresolved otherwise the problem can grow again.

Even though it is difficult to accept, you are the leader of a production (aside from the producers) and you need to take ownership of your vision, every facet of it. Most people have a hard time confronting problems head on, but it's a crucial part of being a great leader on a production, and in life.

Different projects provide different levels of responsibility. Most of the time it has to do with the size of the budget. The bigger the dollar amount the more responsibility a director must have to make sure that the project is completed on time and on budget.

I look forward to the day that I get to direct a hit television series. Being given control of the reins of a series that is loved and respected among industry professionals and fans is a sure way to have an increased sense of responsibility. I think of J.J. Abrams and the nervousness he must have felt when he first started working on *The Force Awakens*. Mind you, that is an enormous franchise and one with a lot of history and clout, but it is a good example of a project that would provide a director with an increased sense of responsibility. It is different for every director I'm sure, but for me I'd love to direct a series. Directing a TV series seems like a bigger task than directing a feature film probably because TV shows tend to be longer projects. Feature films vary depending on the content and budget, but TV shows, if they do well, can go on for years! There's also an added sense of trust when working on a TV series because more often than not, you'll have a handful of different directors work on it. Then it becomes important for each director to keep the style and tone consistent across all episodes.

> "Making a movie and not directing the little moments is like drinking a soda and leaving the little slurp puddle for someoe else."
> - **Steven Spielberg**

I have recognized that my sense of responsibility never changes in importance but only in magnitude. It doesn't matter if I'm directing a micro-budget web series or a multi-million dollar budget feature film, I still have the same level of responsibility as the leader. The only thing that does change is the amount of people and things that I am responsible for (i.e.: magnitude). The size of the budget shouldn't dictate the amount of effort and focus you put into being a leader, it only dictates the amount of people and things you are responsible for. Some would argue that that would mean that you are more or less responsible depending on the budget but I don't see it that way. I will put in just as much effort to be responsible for the success of any low-budget projects I work on as for any big budget projects.

Being responsible also means that you are consistently encouraging those you work with to follow suit. Your behaviour should help dictate that of the crew and cast. When they see you being a kind and ethical person they are automatically thinking about their own actions and how they can contribute to the project in a responsible way. People learn by looking, so when your 1st AD or your boom operator sees you being generous to everyone and making decisions backed by admirable morals they will take notice, and more often than not they will mimic the behaviour. Part of having a team that is responsible for their tasks and behaviour comes back to hiring the right people.

I have a had crew on set that I likely will not hire again because they didn't prove to be effective members of the team that contributed value. They were not responsible leaders in their own right. Laziness and negativity does not go far in my books.

In an ideal world every single team member, whether in a production department or cast would be a positive, enthusiastic, and collaborative player who takes initiative and helps out wherever possible. The reality is that you are going to work with people who fit into the opposite box at some point or another. It is your duty as director to lead them and hopefully change their bad habits, or you'll have to make the hard decisions for the sake of the greater good of the project.

No one ever said that being responsible was easy, but it is necessary if you want to be a successful leader.

INTERVIEW WITH
PAUL SALTZMAN

Prom Night in Mississippi,
The Last White Knight

How did you get into directing?

I never planned to be a filmmaker. I never studied film. I never read a book on filmmaking. I'm the kind of person who is motivated by following my heart in genuine real terms. So I have a dialogue with my own heart and that is a very wonderful facility, if you want to develop it.

How I got into directing was, I had a friend who knew Bo Diddley who was a rock 'n' roll musician who was coming to Toronto and I thought "Woah, that would be cool to film that". It was like "Okay, how do we do this?" I had never done it before. So I went to CBC and I convinced the news department to give me a camera man and a sound man for a day — they were all men in those days. The deal was, they would get a 3-5 minute news item but I would own all the footage for a film of my own, so I was the director and the producer. What motivated me was not "I want to make a film." I've never been motivated by "I'm a filmmaker, I need to make a film."

I had been buying bread at Perlmutter's Bakery in Kensington Market for years. And when you walk into Perlmutter's Bakery it was filled with joy, this bakery was unbelievable. An old Jewish bakery, it had been there for years. The children had taken over and their children didn't want to continue it. It took two years for me to convince them I wanted to make a film of them. Then I had to find the money to do it. It was my first more complex documentary.

And the inspiration was the heart, it wasn't the business, it wasn't the money. Someone said to me once about the film business, "It ain't all sunglasses and autographs kid." So I entered that film in the Canadian Film Awards and to my delight, shock and amazement, it won Best Documentary and Best Director and it won Best Film of the festival. It beat out all the dramas.

Then I was interviewed for the first time in my life. And I remember the interviewer asking "Why do you make the films you make?" And I literally had to pause and ask myself. I said , "I make films about people who give me courage." So it's always about that.

I gave up filmmaking for fifteen years: been there, done that, became a workaholic, ran the third biggest production company in Canada. I did $25 million of production in 1991 – that's like doing $100 million today. I was so busy feeding the machine, paying my 17 employees that I didn't have enough time to see final scripts or see final cuts. So now I work with one assistant out of my home and I love that.

When you think about the word, 'responsibility", what does it mean to you in regards to filmmaking and storytelling?

Well it doesn't mean anything different than that word means to me in every aspect of life. So it's not a specific thing about filmmaking, it's about what the word means. I can answer it from a filmmaking perspective though.

For me, I have never been more joyful in my life than I am now. I am happy now and more delighted with life everyday than I have ever been. Well how does that happen? It doesn't happen with winning awards, it doesn't happen with sunglasses and autographs, it happens by finding that place in your heart and soul where you integrate yourself into a whole human being.

So what does responsibility mean? It means the ability to respond. That's what the word means. I love language because language helps us. If we pay attention to language it assists us. So responsibility is literally the ability to respond. What does that mean? It means, being in the flow, being in your heart, bringing to the people you work with your best self and asking them to bring their best selves.

I learned a couple of great lessons with this on the first drama I ever directed. I've made documentaries, I've won awards, and I had friends who had done dramas, but for some odd reason I had never stepped on a drama set. I had never visited a friend during a shoot. I don't know why, I just hadn't. And the first time I stepped on a drama set I was the director and producer of HBO's premiere episode of their *Family Playhouse* and it remained their top rated episode for five years. I talked my way into it and the person that I had to talk into it believed that I could do it.

So what did I do then? Well the smart thing to do is

to hire the best people. I have hired many directors and it's shocking how often their ego gets in the way of their own creativity.

For me, it's not that way at all. For me, it's a collaborative process, for me it's fun, for me it's play, it's community and communion with the crew and actors and the environment, whether it's a documentary or a drama. So responsibility is how you respond to your community of crew, actors, the environment, the people, including the lowest on the totem pole. How do you treat the first time PA? Well I don't treat the first time PA any different than I treat a star. I actually don't. Why would I? That's kind of sick, right?

I hired the best crew I could for my first drama and I hired Mark Irwin as my director of photography. And how do I know Mark Irwin? I know him because at that time he did all of David Cronenberg's films. Well he's great and I'd seen Cronenberg's films and Cronenberg keeps using him, so he must be pretty cool. I phoned him up and I said "I'm doing this, it's the first time I've done drama. I'm a documentary maker and I want to hire the best people possible and I'd love for you to shoot it. Can we meet?"

We meet and we're on the set the first day, and it's the first setup and it's in a bedroom in a house in the Beaches and I'd done all the storyboards. So I've got it on a clipboard and I'm standing there with Mark and I say "I'd like to do this shot, then we'll go to this shot then this shot," and he does something that you 'don't do' with directors. Very gently, he reaches over and takes my clipboard with my sketches out of my hands and says, "That's great that you've done this.

Now let's just just put that over here," and he puts it on a bureau and he says, "So now we're here in the real situation in the real room. What do you feel like doing?"

That was worth its weight in gold. That was like getting your PHD on your first shot. You have all the backup, but what does it feel like? Responsibility in that moment is the ability to respond. He's saying, "Don't go by a pre-thought way. Be able to respond to what's real here."

Responsibility is a stunningly important piece.

How do you know you're being a responsible and effective leader?

How you know you're being a responsible leader is in the results. Number one, it feels great, to me or to you. The body is this amazing musical instrument and our emotions carry an enormous amount of information. That's what they're for, that's why we have emotions; to have the information, to know what's going on, and to feel wonderful or not.

How do you know you're being an effective, responsible leader?

One, you're feeling really good and creative too.

Two, the people around you are feeling really good.

Three, what you're getting on film or video or whatever your endeavour is, whether you're building a house, making a film, or bringing up a child, you see your results before you eyes.

And those results are creative excellence in harmony, and magic. The magic of creativity.

Is there a project in particular that gave you the biggest sense of responsibility? One for which your ability to respond was at its peak?

When I did *Danger Bay,* I co-created it and produced it. It was very successful. It was Disney, CBC, and Telefilm and no one had ever done a drama like that in Canada. It was like fitting three elephants into a phone booth. The executive from Disney actually said to me one day, "We're Disney and you're not." And CBC wanted their imprint on it, and Disney wanted their imprint and Telefilm had its requirements, and those three groups had never worked together. It was diplomacy, but also creativity, just to get harmony from the three taskmasters.

It took longer to get contracts signed than it normally would because this was all in new territory. We go to the floor and we start shooting because the clients say, "Well we want the episodes now." Well that doesn't mean their contract department is keeping up with them.

There was the first thirteen episodes, which was season one, then we did 22 a year and we did six years so we had 123 episodes, so it was very successful. But in the first year as we're fitting these elephants into the phone booth, twice we were going to run out of money. I thought, "Oh my god, what do we do?" I called everyone together on the floor of the studio. I said, "Look. Here's the situation." Again, it's responsibility, the ability to respond, and it's just truth telling. "We don't have the cash coming in to pay you for the next episode. We will, but it's not here yet. So we can either keep shooting and delay paying you by a week or we could just take next week off without pay. Everyone take a rest, be with your family, do what you want to do. Either way, what we can't do is we can't keep shooting and pay you on time because the money really is not in the bank yet. What would you like to do?" They all asked questions, they were concerned. Then they all said, "We'll take a week off."

I had to do that twice in thirteen weeks because twice the money didn't land in the bank. But the crew felt heard and seen and respected and honoured. So that was one example where it could have been a shit of a mess if I hadn't been upfront. What would have happened if we would have kept shooting and then the checks were delayed? It would have destroyed teamwork, it would have destroyed trust. People would have felt negatively manipulated.

Can you recall a time that you ever had to take responsibility for something that someone else had done because you were the leader on set?

I did a series for CTV and the USA network called *Matrix* which was thirteen one hours. The deal was that the head writers were American and came in from LA. It gets delicate — CTV wants creative control but the USA network wants creative control. So we all agree to sort of share creative control.

The scripts that are being written are far too expensive for the budget. The series was one of the most amazing concepts I ever heard, but wasn't great because we were getting bigger scripts and trying to jerry-rig them down to fit the budget and the time slot. It was a real problem.

On top of that, we had a lead star who was a bit of a loose cannon. We didn't know this when we hired him. People present themselves one way when they want the job and then some people when they have power, and because your star has power just because they're "the star", behave differently. So we never got renewed, we did thirteen hours. Then I find out that everybody's blaming me. The Americans involved, the USA network, their executives, they didn't want to take responsibility that this series with great promise hadn't reached its potential so it's not being renewed. "Well the problem was Paul Saltzman and Sunrise Films." And it's like, "Wait a minute, we went the mile and beyond. We worked so hard with such great people just getting the show done well."

I swear I've never had this experience before, where everyone was bailing out. The CTV executives said, "Well it wasn't me, it was them." And the American partners said, "It wasn't me, it was them." So I was at Cannes and I asked for a meeting with the woman who was then the head of the USA network. Her name is Kay Koplovitz. She is a friend of mine to this day because of what I'm about to tell you, and her right-hand person, David Kenin, is also a friend to this day. I asked for a meeting and we sat down outside in beautiful Cannes during the television festival and I said, "This is not right. It's not right that I'm being blamed and my company's being blamed for the show not being what we all hoped it would be. The reason it's not right is we were getting scripts that were oversized. We had to be manipulating them in the last minute, the scripts were coming in late from the three people that came in from L.A. And they were doing their best, so there's no blame here for anybody, but it certainly isn't my fault and I wouldn't want you to think it is." And they said,

"Well thank you. We respect your courage, we respect your telling us your truth."

That was a situation where what happened was being blamed on me and the only way to deal with that was to tell the truth. Don't trash other people, I didn't trash anybody else. I just said, "Hey, this is not fair, this perception is misplaced." Again, the ability to respond.

What kind of insight would you give to an aspiring director in how to handle someone's bad actions?

I think it goes back to the thing that I mentioned that is the cliché — "The truth will set you free." It happens to be a law of physics.

So how would you as a young director deal with things? Deal with it with truth, not blame. Blame is not truth. If you use truth as a weapon, that's blame. Or if you use lies as a weapon, that's blame.

Check in with yourself, see what your part in the dance is, is there anything that you yourself can shift that will make the situation better? Do that first. Talk to the person or the people that you're not happy with. Talk without blame, examine the situation, "What is going on here? What are you feeling? What is happening? Are we able to do this differently or better."

It's like a dance performance. If everyone isn't dancing to the tune of the music and following the choreography then it's going to be a mess. You don't start shouting at people, you work with them. The way I learned this is you set a level of conscious behaviour and conscious professionalism. You make sure that you hold to that. You don't ignore stuff that isn't okay.

Does the way you respond change on the scale and severity of the situation?

No, it doesn't change at all. The beauty of this is that you come from the heart, you speak truth, you don't blame and denigrate, you work as a team player. Ego has never been my game. I don't like when someone else does it, so when someone else does do it I say "Hey, that doesn't feel good, the way that you're talking to me or the way this is unfolding. How can we do this differently? How can we do this so it does feel good for all of us?" It don't think it matters how small or big it is, it's like physics.

Is there a project that you'd like to work on that would give you an increased sense of responsibility?

No, not really. Everything I do, I do with the same desire for creative excellence. Yeah I have to make money, but the reason I do stuff is never to make money. It's fortunate that I've been able to make money by doing things that I care about.

It's like the glass isn't half full, the glass is already full. Everything I do, I come to it with a sense of devotion, a sense of caring, a sense of responsibility. I wouldn't have more devotion and more caring and more responsibility on project B than project A. The thing about that is that because I don't do projects to make money, I do them to feel fulfilled.

I learned a long time ago in our business, you can either make junk food for the psyche or you can make health food for the psyche. You can make programs that really are shit for people's emotional development, for their emotional body, for their psyche, or you can make beautiful products. So I have never made junk food. When I make something it's because the story turns me on as a human being, it's because the situation needs attention as a human being. Then I bring all of my devotion, all my responsibility, and all of myself to the project.

Have you dealt with projects where you have had to rise up to another level of responsibility and push yourself?

First of all, they're all like that because every project has unique challenges so every one of them requires creativity not just in the production, but creativity in all of the problem solving both behind and in front of the cameras, and from the business end and the manufacturing end. I'd say the biggest stretch that I had to do was when I was hired to work on the first IMAX film which was for the Osaka '70 World Fair. There wasn't even a name yet. There was a contest in the office, there were seven of us, and the contest was who could name what it was going to be called. Eventually it was IMAX.

I was hired to be the researcher, the second unit director and the production manager for a crew of seven. We filmed in ten countries I think. I had to go to fourteen countries and I was 25 years old. I worked literally twenty hours a day, seven days a week. Literally, I slept four hours a night, seven days a week for ten months. And it was a thrill, it was fantastic but I had to do stuff beyond my experience.

Not only did I have to do all the arranging, I had to come up with ideas. The director wanted a compatriot. He wanted someone who could be his righthand person and come up with ideas of what to film, all of which was great for me. That was the most demanding and stretching, but it was a thrill. It was like the job of a lifetime.

What are some actions that aspiring directors can do on a regular basis to ensure that they are responsible leaders?

Well the most powerful tool in creativity is imagination. I know that's easy to say, but imagination is the cornerstone of creativity. So what can anybody do in life, whether they're making film or building a bridge? To use our imagination to foresee it in detail, to do it with joy, to close your eyes and see what it is you want to create then do that with joy.

Allow your creativity to expand. Don't be too controlling. In fact don't be controlling at all. Now this is a tricky word: control. When you're at the control of a car or airplane, you have to be in control, you're controlling it. But in creativity, if we try and pre-think everything…that's where Mark Irwin's lesson comes back.

So creativity is — in a sense the opposite of control. So what can young directors do? See this is the beauty of life. The beauty of life is that the ways to do things are consistent. You want to make a beautiful film? You want to make a beautiful marriage? You want to bring up a beautiful child? You want to create beautiful tapestry? You want to create a beautiful living room? It's all the same. Be in your heart, feel your feelings, let your imagination be free and then implement. And implement responsibility, meaning the ability to respond.

Here's a great story about that. Good friends of mine

wrote and produced Kevin Costner's *Robin Hood*. That was at a time when Kevin Costner was the number one star in Hollywood. And Kevin Costner insisted that Kevin Reynolds be the director. He was a friend of his. The producers, my friends, didn't think he was right for the job, but the superstar says, "I'm not doing it if he doesn't direct it." So they're on the set, and I was actually there. I was visiting with my daughter, it was on the sandy shore of the English Channel. As Morgan Freeman and Kevin Costner pulled themselves out of the water having escaped from the prison in Morocco and they've crossed the English Channel and have dragged themselves out onto the beach, the sheriff comes down the beach with one or two henchmen on horses and there's an altercation.

During the altercation, one of the horses rises up and Kevin Costner, Robin Hood, grabs the reins and the horse goes down on the beach, on the sand. The director wanted a closeup of the horse's head hitting the sand. The camera was down on the ground level, and the object was when he said action the horse handlers, who are masters are it, could get the horse to flop his head down without hurting him. The head flopped down, but it was a little out of frame. The horse handlers said, "Can you move the camera a few inches over here and it will work?" "No!", the director said. And they did twenty four takes. The director refused to move the camera and the horse's head kept dropping not quite in frame. Finally on the twenty fifth take, the director said, "Okay, move the camera," and boom, they got the shot. So there's a lesson in trying to be controlling by dictating, "I'm the director, you will do it my way." In this case, creativity solved the issue in one shot when the director finally let go of control and trusted his experts.

You need to be a director who is willing to receive that collaboration, and whose ego isn't tied to: "I know everything."

6

CONNECT AND UNDERSTAND

TALKING IS A GOOD place to start to connect with your cast and crew. Communication usually solves any problem and when a production starts you're almost always in the situation of not knowing the people who are working with you. When I do my first production meeting with all the key crew members I make a conscious effort to start building a strong connection with each and every person sitting around the table. If it's a smaller project and the first time everyone meets is on the first day of principal photography then I like to take five minutes at the beginning of the shoot to gather the whole team together and have everyone introduce themselves. Then I'll do a short stretch, lead a breathing exercise, or run a game. During production I also make sure to talk to as many people on lunch break as possible because it's a great time to get to know people when they are not under pressure to perform. Do this only assuming your directing duties won't get in the way of taking that time.

You do get to understand and connect with people

Connect And Understand

through the work, but I think it's very important to try and make an effort to know people outside of the work or at least show that you care for them outside of them being there to do their job.

I'm not saying I'm perfect – I've learned that people just want to be acknowledged and appreciated so that is my prime purpose when working with people.

I know that above doing good work is being a good person and part of being a good person is understanding the people who surround you. Take an interest in their life, get to know what motivates them and what their interests are. Depending on the length of the shoot you may have more or less time to do this.

I like to try and ensure that my connections with cast and crew grow overtime, but if I'm being honest, it's not always easy to stay in touch with everyone all the time. I have stronger connections with certain people than others, which is only natural. I do try to reach out to people on important dates like birthdays, anniversaries, etc. When I enjoy working with someone, I want to work with them again, and as I continue to work with the same people on multiple projects, I get to know what their strengths and weaknesses are on a professional level, and I get to know them deeper on a personal level.

> "I think what makes a good actor's director is somebody who understands what I'm doing and is respectful of it, but who also has a vision and is directing me toward their vision in a way that feels productive."
> **- Matt Damon**

I know that the right people come into our lives at the right times because we make it so. When that happens it is our job to make a conscious effort to build connections. Communication is key for keeping connections fresh and luckily with the world today being as connected as it is, it's much easier to create long lasting relationships even at great distances.

Communication comes into play at every moment of every day on set and it is the tool I use to solve each and every problem that may come up. There haven't been too many scenarios where a crew or cast member has had a major problem that had an effect on their performance, but when it does happen I like to do two things.

First I like to have a one-on-one conversation about what is going on – ideally the person who has the problem feels he/she can approach me about it so that I am made aware of their situation because I'm not psychic, so unless I notice something off, it's hard to know what is going on with someone unless they communicate it. When one does communicate their problem to me, I listen, understand and try to find a way to help them cope with whatever is going on whilst doing their job to the best of their ability.

If someone has had a death in the family or something that tends to have quite a profound emotional effect, I often will just tell them to take time to deal with it and rearrange the schedule to be accommodating. Someone should not be expected to jump right back into work, and taking one day off to let the circumstances sink in isn't unreasonable. Thankfully this kind of thing hasn't happened at a time where I had to reschedule something, but I have had to deal with these tough scenarios before. The best thing for me to do is listen and be there as support. Doing anything other than that can cause someone to have an emotional or distressed response which isn't helpful to them, me or the production.

I know that I am more equipped now to handle any sort of situation than I was even two years ago. I have learned a lot about people and how the mind works from amazing teachers, and through that learning I have also gained a lot more insight into myself. I know myself fully and I am aware of my thoughts and emotions. Therefore, I feel like I can successfully enter into any kind of situation and be able to handle myself and help other people involved. There have been times when I've had to be a source of stability and calmness when one or more people on set are feeling anxious or distressed. The last thing I want to do in those situation is feed into the emotions as it will only amplify the tension.

WHEN PROFESSIONAL LIFE BECOMES PERSONAL

As a leader you want to work at keeping your current relationships strong and make an effort to forge new ones. You never know which ones will turn into lifelong friendships.

There are a handful of people that I have grown closest with over the years. In the last five years or so I have become good friends with Tiffanie Caracassis whom I actually met through LinkedIn, believe it or not. She and I have worked a lot together, mainly on *Out Of Frame*, but she has also been instrumental in the capacity of a production manager and on-screen talent on several other projects. She is smart, super organized and I trust her to get the job done. Tiffanie is also just an amazing person to have around because she is so bubbly and sweet and makes everyone around her smile. I always look forward to working with Tiffanie regardless of what the project is. She and I have become true friends over the last few years and I am so happy to have her in my life. To use her words, "together we will conquer the world!" She is one of those people that always has high energy. She is a joy to be around and helps keep me level-headed when things get stressful. It's at the point where we have a shorthand so it almost seems like we can read one another's minds.

I have been working very closely with a friend of mine who I met while at Ryerson, Katie Favrin. I helped her launch her YouTube channel, *Q&A with Lady K*, and I have been acting as a co-producer, videographer, and editor for her channel as well. Katie and I first worked together when I needed someone to be on-camera and conduct interviews at the second annual Canadian International Television Festival in Toronto. She saved my butt and it made my job much easier because I didn't have the stress of having to come up with questions as well as produce and film the interviews. Since that first event, our friendship has grown and I have asked Katie to participate as the interviewer at several other events including the Buffer Festival, nextMEDIA, and the CMAO Awards.

Thomas Peever and I have become closer since we first met in university because while we did have classes together and worked on several projects together, Thomas has been an integral part of my production company since its inception. He was there when I had my first team meeting, he wrote dozens of reviews for the *SLP Movie Watchlist*™, and he and I have been developing a drama television series together since the summer of 2012. Thomas and I push one another creatively and we support one another a lot so it's always fun working with him. I can't wait to develop more awesome projects with him in the future!

Having worked on *Revolution 10* for the last few years, I have also grown quite close with Sonja Verpoort, the screenwriter. Both Sonja and I have learned a lot about feature film development and interactive storytelling, as well as a lot about one another while working on it together. It has been a thrill working with her on the project and we cannot wait to share it with the world! I also directed a dark comedy short film that she wrote and produced called *Dinner With Bernice*, which was a super fun experience. Sonja is a writer that I definitely want to continue to work with. She has become a great friend and I genuinely care about her personal and professional well-being.

There are also many other cast and crew members as well as other writers that I have worked with over the years that I would work again with in a heartbeat (you know who you are). I care about the people who take the time to create stories with me and I want them to be super successful in their endeavours.

I know that when people want to come back to work with me on projects that I must be doing something right in terms of my interpersonal skills. I like to think I am an approachable person. It's impossible to please everyone, but I am conscious of my behaviour so even in situations where my patience is tested I have more control over my reactions to things that happen. I know that if I keep myself in check and stay humble, I'll always consider myself to be approachable.

CONNECTING IN SOCIAL SCENARIOS

I think that socializing with colleagues outside of work is definitely important. The amount of time spent doing so depends a lot on the schedule and the workload and everyone's roles, but I don't see an issue with it if it means bringing people closer together.

If and when any socializing becomes distracting or hinders performance and/or professionalism, that's when ground rules may need to be put in place, though I've never had to resort to that and I hope I never do.

Wrap parties and other production related social events are great times to connect with cast and crew on a different level even though it is somewhat work related. It's nice to see people let loose a bit and open up more when there isn't any pressure to work. On the flip side I think that it's important for everyone (including myself) to stay aware and be professional even in a social situation. While I don't think that a crew member drinking too much in front of me is grounds for firing them, I do think that what is said or done while intoxicated needs to be top of mind because substances like alcohol can make one say or do things that may not have been said or done otherwise. It's just a matter of balance I think. Go out and party and have fun, but keep in mind that if you are with colleagues certain

> "Film is incredibly democratic and accessible, it's probably the best option if you actually want to change the world, not just re-decorate it."
> **- Banksy**

things that happen in a social scenario can bleed through or have an impact on what happens in a professional or work environment. No matter what kind of social gathering you take part in people will still see you as the director, so be conscious of the way you behave.

SUPPORT SYSTEMS AND UNDERSTANDING

I think it's in every director's best interest to surround themselves with people who care as much about their leader as their leader does about them. You want to create an environment that nurtures a supportive team that will reciprocate the effort you put in. There have been times when I've cracked under pressure and the cast and crew have come together to help me out of whatever slump I was temporarily experiencing. I vividly remember having a hard time when I was in high school and I was directing plays. As it got closer to the show, I was feeling the pressure and sometimes I let it get to me in front of everyone. Of course I know better now to take a moment to myself and pull myself together, but when I first started directing I didn't fully know who I was, so in high stress scenarios I allowed my anxiety to take over and didn't react the way I should have.

I learned from those experiences and I recognize that when one dumps their problems onto others, it can do one of two things: it can push people away and have them not take you as seriously, or it can create friction, both of which can have profound effects on the success of the project and the people working on it.

It all turned out well in the end, but looking back knowing

what I know now about conflict resolution and about myself, I would have carried myself differently. Live and learn, as they say.

Speaking of learning, over the course of working on a variety of productions, I have picked up on some of the easier and more effective ways to connect with others. Below I've listed a few of them. They may seem blatantly obvious, but it's funny how most of us forget to do these things consciously.

1. When talking with someone, ask about them. Be interested, not interesting. Listen to them when they talk about what is happening in their lives outside of the production and ask specific follow up questions to show that you do in fact care and are listening. It's not to say that you have to talk to people all day because you'd never get the shooting done, but just be aware of the moments where you can take time to learn more about your team members.

2. Learn every cast and crew member's name and only call them by their name. It is truly amazing how big of a difference this makes in communication and how much it means to people to be addressed by their first name. Communication is also a lot faster when you make the effort to do this.

3. Show your team that you care. Take time to ask how their day is going, find a moment to tell your crew how much you love and appreciate their hard work. Write personalized 'thank you' cards for every single cast and crew member for the wrap of the production. Do any-

thing you can to show the people who are putting in their blood, sweat, and tears to help bring your vision to life that you care about them. You would not be able to accomplish anything without them.

Showing appreciation and support is one of the best ways to connect with and understand the team you work with. You never know what awesome facts you'll learn about people and I can guarantee that you'll not only grow potentially life-long relationships, but you'll also have a more fruitful working environment.

> **– BONUS –**
> Visit **beyondthedirectorschair.com/bookbonus** to download 5 tips for finding the right team.

INTERVIEW WITH
SPENCER MAYBEE

Carmilla,
Letterkenny

Why did you decide to get into film?

I used to write when I was quite young and I also used to perform, but it wasn't until I was in high school and I saw *Miller's Crossing* for the first time that I wanted to get into the film industry. It's a gangster film set in the prohibition era in some ambiguous town. For me it was one of the finest cohesions of all the arts of cinema in one film. I watched it a lot and I strangely took solace in it. That was the movie that made me want to be a director because I realized that I was not particularly good at any one thing but that I was medium good at a lot of things and that possibly my best potential would be in bringing together people and talents in many different fields to create something that is better than the sum of its parts.

What was your first directing experience?

When I was in university I made a little short film. A team of people and I worked on this screenplay and I can't even remember what it was about, but we made it and then we had to edit it deck to deck, which was horrid. That was probably my very first, and then I made a film when I lived in Winnipeg.

The film community in Winnipeg is really supportive. You end up working with all of these great union crews and they were talented like most union crews but still a small enough community that there wasn't any of the jaded attitudes that you get sometimes in bigger cities with bigger union crews. You got these great people and they were super professional and really happy, really good at their work and wanted to help out, lending their hands to small independent productions. There was a bit of a boom of some really cool, well produced films coming out of Winnipeg at the time.

What do you do to connect with your crew and cast?

Typically I like to have a script read through within prep so everybody can kind of get a clear sense of whats going on because everybody is at the table at the same time. Then the cast can relax and go elsewhere and all your keys can sit down and talk about the script together. Usually at that meeting is when I would be like 'hey guys, welcome to the team', ask for everybody to introduce themselves, say a little bit of a statement about what we're trying to do, and get everybody on the same page.

Sometimes it's easy to get jaded and I think sometimes what happens is filmmakers can quickly forget what they're doing and who they're doing it for. That's a recipe for a divisive set. You end up working against production instead of having production working for you.

The more sets that you're on, the more people that you meet that work in the business and so the more you get a sense of personalities and how you jive. Once you find a team of people that you at least get along with and you can rely on professionally then the next step is trying to see if you can have a creative collaboration. In some departments, that's more important than others. You definitely want to make sure that you and the screenwriter are seeing the world of the film in similar ways.

If you're new to film and you don't have a friend in every department then I think the trick is really to get on as many sets as you can and challenge yourself to be personable and get to know people. A lot of people go to film school and that's how they meet other people. Some people reach out to communities like LIFT and small co-ops where filmmakers can help each other out. I think that the real trick is just to get on sets and sometimes you have to do a bit of that before you can reach out and pull favours and ask people to come and help on your thing. That's the 'paying your dues' thing that some people talk about.

How do you ensure that your connections with the cast and crew grow overtime, even after the production is done?

Everybody in the business works on a lot of productions and if you have a really good time with somebody and you really connect on set, great - but it's hard to get together and everybody wants to have a drink with everybody. I think that is one of the reasons why people see our industry as a party industry. It's strange, but those parties serve a really important function, as do wrap parties. You know a lot of people skimp on wrap parties or forget about them or it's easy to forget about them, especially on a divisive set, because on a divisive set the last thing you want to do is hang out with people that you've been arguing with for the last three weeks.

Little ceremonies are important. You know when you wrap an actor on a set you should announce it and the crew should like say goodbye to them and typically the crew gives a round of applause for the actor for their performance. It's strange that we don't do that for key crew, but that's usually because key crew all wrap at the same time. And at that point, that's when you have a big round of applause for everybody on the crew, and a wrap party.

I'm not advocating for a party lifestyle. You don't even have to get wasted or anything. The point is that it serves a function.

When a crew or cast member is having a problem, what do you say or do to be understanding of their situation?

Typically, I try to go on the principal of 'praise in public, criticize in private'. If somebody is having difficulty I think discretion is really important, especially with actors, they are very exposed and very vulnerable.

If there's a specific problem, or if someone is having an issue with somebody else, or if something's wrong and you don't know what it is, you just have to take them aside and try to find a production appropriate time to do that.

Usually at the source of any sort of issue it's either a personal thing or it's a creative thing. If it's a creative thing there's a conversation that needs to be had. If it's a personal thing then depending of the nature of it on one side or the other of that disagreement or that discord, somebody needs to professional-the-hell up.

Sometimes it's just a matter of people disagreeing in terms of how they work. As a professional you have to understand that people work in different ways. This is where keeping the eyes on the prize is really important or remembering who your audience is.

I worked in a situation where a cast member felt like their character would have very different wardrobe choices than what we had in the budget. That became a discussion between the wardrobe department and myself and the cast and the producers because we just didn't really have a lot of money to pull together. What it ended up coming back to was that we needed to dig a little bit deeper and push to find more options that were cheaper but didn't look cheap. It's all just creative solutions at that stage of the game.

I had a situation on another set where I had an AD who was filling in. He came on late in the game and just came off a big show and was very stressed and didn't have the flexibility that an AD needs to have on a set to work around things.

The important thing is keep the team on track and carry on. It's important to cover for people like that in those times and deal with them separately (praise in public, criticize in private) and you just carry on. You work without the team member if you need to.

There's a whole different world that happens when you have a budget and when you don't. When you have a significant budget where the amount of money that you're offering people is enticing enough, they're willing to make creative or personal sacrifices. In leadership roles you can be a dictator and you can say: "shut up and do it or you're fired!".

I don't like that attitude and that's not the attitude that I want but in some cases I think that is the attitude that people afford when they pour money into something. A lot of people are not necessarily strong in interpersonal communication, and so their communication comes down to "do it or you're fired" and that's how they know how to deal with problems.

That's an expensive way to do things. Whereas if you work to bring together teams of likeminded individuals who are collaborating on a piece of art together, it could be just like a cheap rom-com or something, but as long as all of you buy into the ultimate payoff for your audience then I think it can be less adversarial.

Sometimes you have to be ready to fight for things creatively but you don't want to fight dirty. I think it's important to fight according to rules and to do so by to just demonstrating how you feel and what you think about things.

What have you said or done in the past that has had a positive response or outcome?

I worked with an actress that was really struggling when I was giving direction and there was a certain degree of the natural insecurity that goes with being an actor and being emotionally exposed in front of a lot of people. I could tell there was confusion. What I needed to do was figure out how can I communicate better. What I was getting from the performance was just melodramatic and what I wanted was a bit more of a toned down, understated, naturalistic performance. I needed to find the right words so that we were using the same vocabulary.

One of the key things that I think is important in communicating with performers is reminding them that you're shooting many takes, you're trying to get options, so you're not saying 'that was terrible', you know. Sometimes you can call it out, but you have to be tender and sensitive.

You pull the actor aside if you're struggling with getting a performance and sometimes they'll have a creative reason and that's a creative discussion. Sometimes what they're doing is they're trying to give you what you want, but they're unable to get there, and that becomes just a communication conversation.

If I felt entitled to give advice to a younger or a newer director I would say check yourself. Chances are you're the one who is not communicating well. It's your job to get the result.

Who are the people you have grown closest with over the years? What were their positions or roles in the production?

I have some writer/filmmaker friends who I'm quite close with. We co-wrote a script together and made that into a movie and bonded through that process. I have friends that I know from film school. I went to the CFC and I have many friends from that, several of them are editors. Two closer friends are writers, and part of that is because I worked with them. You know, you work closely with somebody, you end up kind of jiving, and you have a good sort of discourse. I have a tendency to like actors, I find them fascinating and interesting and I like the variety of perspectives that they can bring.

I had a really great collaboration on *Carmilla* with my DP, Rob Walsh. In some ways when you have a great collaboration it's really uplifting.

For me a great collaboration is when as a director you're able to communicate your vision, and they come to the table with other artistic ideas.

What are your thoughts on spending time with cast and/or crew outside of work hours during a production? Do you think it is better to keep things professional while a production is going on?

I think it's great if you can. I think it's important to try and maintain those connections. It's about allowing that relationship to potentially flourish and build because maybe you're going to have a conversation, maybe you'll get ideas. If you like the people, hang out with them.

I'm not going to hang out with everybody that I work with on set, but that doesn't mean that I don't like them. And everybody is busy.

It really depends on the schedule and the timeline that you're working on. I always want to respect that the people that I'm working with have personal lives. I never feel weird if people don't want to hang out. Usually if I'm directing something then one hundred percent of the focus is on the thing, so the rest of my life kind of takes a back seat to it. I don't have time to go get a beer with the crew because I need to be figuring out my shot list for tomorrow. It's pretty rare that I have a moment at lunch, just to call my wife to be like 'hey, how's your day going?'.

Based on past experiences, would you consider yourself to be an approachable person? Why or why not?

Yeah, I think I'm a pretty approachable person. It's funny, you know I realize there are aspects to a director's career where it's important to seem cool. I think sometimes one of the parts of the collateral damage of appearing cool or being cool is that you can appear unapproachable. You can come off as too cool for school, and then nobody at school wants to talk to you.

What are your best qualities when it comes to understanding other people and their situations?

I think empathy is a big one. It helps me understand because I think I'm good understanding other people's perspectives and that's part of why I got into writing - I can imagine myself into the headspace and the emotional space of people in very different circumstances than my own. I value listening and I value being empathetic, so I think those are my strengths.

I also care about words and I care about the meaning of words. I went to university for poetry, which is a very weird degree to get, but part of the reason is because I love language and there are many subtle nuances.

In the film industry I've tried to work in as many different departments so that I can understand the impact of small decisions on every department, because if you want to be a leader of people I think you need to understand where they're coming from. I knew that I wanted to be a director so I knew that it would only be to my benefit to get a bit of experience in as many different departments as possible so that you win a little bit of respect from that crew. They will move mountains for you if you demonstrate yourself as worthy, if you care about them.

Sometimes you can't do that. Sometimes you have to bone your crew a little bit for creative reasons, but if I'm ever going to do that, I'm going to make an announcement on set. If you can appeal to their sense of creative pride anybody on a film set can get behind that, but they can't get behind it if you don't communicate it to them.

Often what happens is your AD will pick up the leadership slack and sometimes that needs to happen because the director has a lot of other work to do between set ups. You need a great AD who recognizes that leadership and can rally the troupes and appeal to the crew while you're doing your business.

If you've been gifted an opportunity, you have almost even more responsibility to demonstrate that you deserve it, or that you're the right person for that job. You demonstrate to the people that are on your set that you have vision, that you're a responsible leader, and that you're going to steer the ship and not lead them with stupid decision-making.

To be fair to many crews, they work on a lot of shows and a lot of crew members have more experience on set than a lot of directors. As a director I think you owe your crew that respect.

I don't tolerate any douche-baggery on my set, you know, people being snotty to other people in departments. It's not cool. I don't want that person on my set. I don't want sexists, I don't want racists, and I don't want people who can't manage themselves with any degree of appropriate behaviour. I want people who know how to control their language. Sometimes I let that go a little and I have to catch myself, but I want to make sure that I'm not worried about other people so I can worry about myself.

Have you had a past experience where someone on the production has connected with you and was understanding of a situation you were going through?

Typically, 100% of your experience as a director (if you've got a decent crew and a great cast) is everybody is sensitive to what you're going through because they're all working to help you build this thing that you designed. Some of the design comes from the screenwriter and some of the design comes from the director.

Carmilla had a really crazy shoot schedule: 190 pages in four days. We didn't have flexibility to extend our days. We didn't have the room to go into overtime for budgetary reasons, but also we were shooting in an apartment that was in a residential place. We couldn't go into the night because there were upstairs and downstairs neighbours who had to work the next morning so we had to work it within the waking hours of the day.

So one morning we show up and all the lights that we had rigged in the ceiling had fallen. Miraculously, no damage was done, but I was like 'Oh, shit! That's at least a half-hour relight that we need to do plus fixing the set once they're out of there'. That's at least 45 minutes of time that I just lost in my day, which is insignificant on a normal day, but when you're trying to get fifty pages in a day, it's kind of crazy.

I called Rob in. He saw it and the way that he handled it gave me extreme confidence. Rob saw it, he didn't freak out, he didn't react like it was a big deal. He saw that it was something that needed addressing right away and he handled it so smoothly that I instantly had that stress relief.

I've worked on sets where you will find people who will amplify stress, they will take a stressful thing and make it bigger and spread it. You'll find people who will take a stressful thing and not amplify it but pass it along. And then you'll find people who will sink the stress. They'll see something and take care of it. Those are the people you want to work with.

If you feel stressed, your number one job is to not pass it on. Manage your own shit, don't pass it on to others, and react with a sober mind. When you're the director, a lot of the time you don't know exactly what needs to happen, so you need to talk to the department head. That's where being calm and communicative is really important.

Any other comments or stories that you would like to add?

Making films and making movies and even making TV shows is about connecting with others and understanding others. If you don't have that as a core value, maybe you shouldn't be in the industry.

Build up your empathy, build up your communication skills. You gotta know what's up to a certain degree and you have to have ideas, but I think everybody universally responds to someone who is an open collaborator, especially as a director.

It's very easy to think of the director as supposed to be the best at everything, but in fact I think it's way better if the director is not the best at everything. Maybe that's just self-serving but I want to be surrounded by people who are the best at their thing.

As a director, my job is to make sure that everybody in every position is proud of that film. That's when I've done my job. If I can do my job in such a way that my actors are getting awards for their performances, or that my DP is getting awards for his cinematography, that's my big win.

I think ultimately your job is to make beautiful films. Some people go at that differently.

If you're meeting people that you've never met before and trying to figure out in a short period of time whether or not you guys are going to have a creative connection, and possibly be able to work together, how they come prepared to that first meeting and how prepared I am to that first meeting is going to dictate the dynamic of that relationship. What I expect from anybody is that they come prepared to that meeting with ideas, thoughts and openness, and with an experience that they can draw upon. I want to have a sense moving forward that I'm working with somebody who is going to have solutions.

What I'm looking for in terms of creative collaborators, are people who can play their position well. This is tying back to a sports metaphor but you don't want a goalie who is really good at penalty kicks, because he's not going to be taking a lot of them. You want a goalie who is good at saving penalty kicks, who is good at stopping balls.

Certain skills lend themselves to certain departments really well and you want to make sure that the people that you're putting in those positions are good at those things. It sounds like a sweeping generalization, but in that first meeting people need to demonstrate that because if they don't recognize that as an opportunity to demonstrate their professionalism or their talent or skill, then they're not going to recognize other opportunities.

You do have to trust your gut, but these are the little details that happen in the meeting.

7

TAKE ON CHALLENGES

THE DESIRE AND ABILITY to take on challenges is part of what I know will allow me to be continuously successful, not just in directing, but in life. Before we get into it, you have to ask yourself one question:

Do you enjoy taking on challenges?
If your answer is 'yes', then answer this question:
Do you actively seek out new challenges?

If you answered 'yes' again, then you are well on your way to being a super successful director if you aren't one already.

If you answered 'no' to either one of those questions, then hopefully this chapter will change your viewpoint on challenges.

People don't take on challenges for various reasons. Maybe they feel they are too inexperienced, maybe they need more money, maybe they need more equipment, maybe they need the right connections, or maybe they are just scared of failing. There are a billion reasons we give ourselves for not taking on a challenge. I know because I do it too sometimes. Even for me it can take someone else lighting a fire under my butt for me to get motivated to just go for it.

It happens to all of us. The trick is how fast we can forget about the excuses for not taking on a challenge and how often we can work past the pushbacks.

For those of you who did answer 'no' to the two questions I asked previously, and even if you answered 'yes', I want to give you ten steps you can follow to help you be more willing to take on challenges. If you follow these ten steps you will be at least ten percent closer to overcoming the challenge that will catapult you forward one thousand miles.

While these steps are associated with directing, they can apply to all things.

Step 1: Think about something that you want to do but haven't, or a challenge that you want to take on that you haven't taken on. The key is knowing that you haven't done it yet. It doesn't mean that you'll never do it. Writing it down will hopefully bring it into the foreground for you.

Step 2: Write down all the reasons you haven't done it yet. These can be any reason, no matter how small or large.

Step 3: Next to all the reasons you wrote in Step 2, write down if you think they are under your control or not. You can write C for the ones under your control, and NC for the ones not in your control. We all make up excuses and create limitations for ourselves so this is a way to weed out which ones are actually under your control and which ones aren't.

Step 4: Look at the ones you wrote C next to. Are there

more of those than there are of the ones you wrote NC next to? If so, you're on the right track because you have just proven to yourself that you have more control over the challenge than you may have thought.

Step 5: Go back and look at the ones you wrote NC next to. Look at them again and see if you can change the NC to C. Really give them a good look and decide which of those are not under your control. Did you change some of them?

Step 6: Affirm that you have control. Say aloud, "I have control over (challenge you want to overcome) and I can accomplish it!" Now that we've established that you have control over the challenge and can take it on, let's get into how you are actually going to do that.

Step 7: Go back and read over what you wrote in Step 1. Write down the first thing you can do about it. It should be something simple and something that you can implement with confidence right away.

Step 8: Write down everything you can think of to do to be able to complete the challenge. Think of them as all the small steps you need to climb to reach the top of the staircase.* Take as much time as is needed to do this.

Step 9: Implement the first thing you wrote down in Step 7. How did it make you feel? Fill in the blank: "I want to (challenge I want to overcome) and I just (what you just implemented) so I am now (*remaining number of steps) closer to achieving my goal."

Step 10: Look back at the comprehensive list of steps you need to follow. Put them in order. Make a schedule to check each one off. Get excited because you are already much closer to overcoming your challenge.

Once you have completed the ten steps let me know if they helped you. Email your stories to leah@leahrifkin.com – I want to hear them!

This ten step process allows you to confront the challenges you were too afraid to confront. Often fear is the main thing that holds us back from actually doing things that we are totally capable of doing. Once you can prove to yourself that you are capable of taking on any challenge that comes your way, it is much easier to get excited about new and even bigger challenges.

Speaking of challenging projects that I am excited about... I am stoked to take on *Revolution 10* which would be my biggest and most ambitious project to date. Directing an interactive feature film is super appealing to me simply because of the amount of problems I'm going to have to solve and the amount of things I will learn in doing so.

I actively seek out projects that challenge me as a director because what else is there to do? I mean what is the point in doing the same projects over and over without trying anything new. And I don't mean that the entire format has to be different, even if it's just a different genre or an interesting

> "I love the incredible variety of demands directing makes on you, from the entrepreneur to the hustler to the deal-maker to the writer; to directing actors and the camera and working with music, sound, marketing and promotion. It uses so many sides of your brain."
> **- Tom Hooper**

story that comes with a set of physical challenges or challenging camera angles. Even though I direct two very different web series doesn't mean they don't both present challenges on various levels. The content does not usually dictate the amount of challenges, nor their magnitude.

I know I don't have any limitations in terms of what I am capable of doing as a director. I am pretty much game to direct anything from animated films to bloody war scenes. I do have limitations from an ethical standpoint. For example, I would never force an actor to get into a situation they weren't comfortable with and that they hadn't agreed upon beforehand in the contract. I would never ask cast or crew member to do anything that put their physical, mental, or emotional health at a detrimental risk. Anyone who has ever worked on a production knows that there is always some level of physical, mental or emotional challenges, but none that aren't insurmountable. I would also never harm animals.

I digress.

Challenging projects bring the most reward, and not always in the form of cash. Putting money aside, what is key to note is what happens to you when you do something that challenges you.

When you take on a challenge, you:

1. Get excited immediately.

2. Want to start working on it right away.

3. Want to tell others about the amazing thing you're working on.

4. Are constantly motivated to do more with the challenge.

5. Want it to get harder. – It's backwards, but it's true.

6. Don't lose sight of the overall goal and the end result.

7. Don't want to stop until you've overcome the challenge.

8. Are excited to talk about it when people ask about it.

9. Love the challenge and want more.

These are generalizations, but I can guarantee that these apply to every scenario, even ones that are not related to directing.

The above nine things happened to me, and are still happening to me with regards to *Revolution 10*. It's my biggest challenge yet and it's so exciting! Many people think I am out of my mind and most people think the project is not real. Though I guess I can understand why a perfect stranger might think that an interactive feature film controlled by your brainwaves sounds a bit like science-fiction.

Taking on challenges is part of the game of life. For me directing is only fun when I'm doing something that challenges me. The fun is in getting up in that challenge's face and saying: "Bring it on."

Recently I directed a short film that I submitted into the TIFFxInstagram Festival. The sequence of events happened in the exact order as above. I heard about the festival from my dad, got very excited as soon as I read about it, and I immediately decided I wanted to submit to it. I told people I knew that I was submitting to it and was so motivated to get an idea going that I started brainstorming ideas. I wanted to make it more challenging for myself so I decided to write it so that you don't know what the short is about until the very end. Throughout the whole process of filming and editing it, I always had the end result in mind. I knew the tone of the whole film upon inception of the concept, before I even started writing. After I submitted it I was excited when people asked me about it. Oh, and I did the whole thing from concept to submission within a seven day period. I loved working on it so much and was on such a high from overcoming the challenge that I wanted to immediately start on another challenge.

Working on the short film for the TIFFxInstagram Festival definitely improved me as a director because I did three things one hundred times better than I ever have before. Firstly, I was a thousand times more organized than previous shoots so the whole shoot took less than three hours. Secondly, because I was so prepared I felt confident to be extremely decisive. I made decisions faster than I ever have. And lastly, I was not overly concerned about the small details. I was aware of them but I didn't get stressed or worried about them. The saying 'don't sweat the small stuff' definitely applied. The reason I didn't worry about them was because I knew. I just knew that it would all turn out exactly the way I envisioned it. That was the first time I was able to let go on set and just enjoy the process. It was such a freeing moment.

It is at this point in the chapter where I should remind you

> "There are no rules in filmmaking. Only sins. And the cardinal sin is dullness."
> - Frank Capra

that some of the strategies I am giving you and the lessons I am sharing are things that I have learned from role models and mentors. Coaches and mentors are great resources for successfully overcoming challenges because that is their job. They are there to challenge you, guide you through the process, and validate your success at the end. I have had so many mentors but there is one person in particular that pushed me to challenge myself. I'm talking about my high school drama teacher and mentor, Mr. Hosios. He is a wonderful person. I was always thrilled to go to his class because it was the only class where I was truly excited to take on challenges.

I remember in Grade 10, we had a performance of a monologue that was worth a large portion of the final grade. I ended up writing a monologue based on the story of the main character in a French-Canadian film called *Aurore*. It was a very emotional monologue in which my character was talking about being beaten by her step-mother. I practiced and practiced and I knew all my lines, but the challenge for me was crying at the end. I went to Mr.Hosios for support and he knew that I could overcome my challenge, but I had to prove it to myself. Before I got up on stage to perform it, I took a deep breath and lost myself in the performance. It was only when I stopped trying so hard and just confronted it that I was I able to cry. I balled my eyes out.

Then in my senior year at Langstaff Secondary School I co-directed two plays. As mentioned in the introduction, one was a short one act play and the other was a full length play. These were my first directing experiences and they were moments I will cherish for the rest of my life even though they were, at that time, the biggest challenges I had ever taken on. Mr. Hosios allowed me to stumble and fall and encouraged me to get back up on my own and figure out the solution to the problem. He was a great support in learning about directing actors, blocking, and making all elements of the production come together to tell a powerful and engaging story.

I'll never forget my time in his drama class and everything he taught me. I feel blessed that I was able to learn from him.

CLOSE YOUR EYES, AND JUMP!

My best piece of advice is to strive to do things that scare you. Every time I have gone out of my comfort zone, the best results have come. The key is also to not care so much about the outcome of what you're doing. By letting go of any expected results you allow the universe to just take care of things. You've done what you need to do and the rest will happen on its own. You put the wheels in motion and after a while they'll start to turn on their own, so to speak.

Another tip would be to do any necessary preparation and research before diving into a challenge. The more prepared you are the easier it will be to try things with actors or with new shots and the less worried you'll be about messing up.

Taking on creative challenges forces you to take on personal challenges in focus, stamina, and resilience. If you can persevere with challenges you set for yourself then you will have no issue taking on challenges that others may set for you. This is true whether they be writers who give you a complex script to bring to life, or producers, who will ask you to accomplish unbelievable feats with limited time and money. It's also true with actors, who will ask you to look at a scene differently than how you imagined through their performances, or mentors, who will test you until your breaking point and beyond.

Get started. Grab hold of the next challenge that comes your way, stare it in its metaphorical eyes, and take it down!

INTERVIEW WITH
KEN GIROTTI

Vikings, Daredevil, Orphan Black, Pure, Rescue Me, ReGenesis

What's the biggest challenge that you've taken on to date?

Well, I can quantify that a lot of different ways. It could be a very big scene with a lot of complex logistical stuff happening in it or it could be a pivotal dramatic scene that's vital to the story. But I would say the biggest challenge I've taken on as a director is more like the biggest challenge that anyone could take on, which is taking on a vocation that requires a certain level of dedication. I suppose the biggest challenge I've faced as a director oddly enough, is deciding to continue to direct.

This was a number of years ago. I was young, I wanted to do what everyone else wanted to do as a director and it was before I completely understood what it takes to have a life in this business. It takes about 10% talent and 90% persistence. The number of amazingly talented people I've seen go by the wayside is remarkable. In my case I was lacking in the persistence department. I felt I had tried and tried and tried and had had some success, and a good share of failures as well.

I found myself at a point of my career where I just couldn't get enough work to survive. So it was bit of an epiphany where I realized that I had to decide whether I wanted to continue banging my head against what felt like a brick wall, or whether I should just stop and turn left, right or backwards into something completely different, or perhaps not as difficult. I considered all of my options and still, the only one that made sense was the option I'd originally chosen. Faced with the challenge of moving forward or completely changing the course of what I wanted to do, I decided to keep at it. I realized that the fire in my belly that had been there since the beginning hadn't really gone out, so I redoubled my efforts.

Everything I did to get my next directing gig had nothing to do with directing, but it did help me sharpen the tools a bit. I did get my next gig and I did better. I got another gig after that and the snowball kind of took off. I still remain paranoid and nervous to this day about where my next job's going to come from. But I've grown up a bit, just a bit, and I have a sort of Stockholm syndrome relationship with that side of things, the paranoia and self-worth slip that can get to any freelance artist. I try not to let it govern my state of being or take over my mood... most of the time. Here I am, I'm doing what I want to do, and have been for quite a while. But I had to go through the challenge that this line of work presented: was I up to it? I guess I was.

To other forms of challenges, I had some directing challenges on a little TV movie I did years ago called *Mayerthorpe*. It was about a few mounties who were murdered by a guy who many people considered crazy. It took place in rural

Alberta. The story became deeply important to me. I had taken emotional possession of it and that can present its own set of challenges.

Sometimes it can be difficult to communicate what one's 'take' on material is. I mean that's part of the challenge of the job, but sometimes even when you communicate effectively you find that because others who have a stake in the material have different objectives, they may not understand your language, or more precisely the language of directing and storytelling. It can be a challenge to hold on to the essence of a film or television show when there are so many other individuals involved.

I had gotten a little reductive and decided it was a story of good versus evil. I interpreted the story in terms of a question: "How bad does a really good person have to get in order to catch a really bad person?" Everything flowed from that, the look, the tone, the framing, the production design, the cutting, the score...all of it. I realized that for one of the few times in my career I had climbed way out on a limb, and with somebody else's money I was all in, hanging by my little finger.

That's a convoluted way of saying that I found myself with a clear vision for the piece and my producing partners and the writer were all on board, but it became a challenge to satisfy other concerned parties. In the end it all worked out, and we ended up with something I'm very proud of. I ended up getting the cast I really wanted and I ended up being in a position where I was working with two producers who were incredibly supportive. We still had to fight the good fight with the network for the creative sovereignty over the project and what I, we, really thought it was about, but we all, the network included, came to the same place, and it was good. But it was challenging.

I've had other challenges that have had to do more with logistics, or the puzzle side of filmmaking. I suppose I like to think what actors do with words in the right setting with the right lighting and production design supporting them, and a decent director, is the alchemy of the job. I kind of think that's where a lot of the 'artistry' of it resides. There's great art in the, what I'd call, the puzzle or the maze of storytelling, with things like action sequences or montages or car chases or anything of a slightly higher concept. There are the challenges that are more 'nuts and bolts' to a degree, like sequences that require deeper logistical and creative planning, storyboards, big rigging jobs, things like that.

I had a battle scene in season three of *Vikings*, which was the biggest battle scene they had ever even conceived of on that show. (They've since eclipsed that.) Even the stunt coordinator said that it was bigger than anything he and his crew had done on *Braveheart*. And we were doing a bloody TV show.

It's one thing to do a battle scene for its own sake, but ultimately you have to ask what the battle is really about? And that question for me is, "What's the story I'm trying to tell in this battle scene?" The challenge was that I was trying to show how much more tactically astute this British king is than this Viking leader is. What that led to in terms of storytelling was another question: "What happens when a leader, who everybody has every confidence in, fails miserably? What happens to him?" That was the story or the query, ultimately that that battle had to serve. But that battle was barely half the episode so it became "How do I render battle tactics as a way of storytelling?" That was a challenge. And I think we were successful.

So those were three types of challenges — one being personal, one being creative and another being nuts-and-bolts directing.

Would you say that you have limits in terms of things you'd never do or lines you'd never cross, on any level, whether it's personal or logistical or story wise?

Yeah, I would suppose I have an ethical limit. Although I've never come across it. For example, I suppose I'd look at some of the films like the *Saw* franchise or any kind of torture porn that's out there and say that's not really my cup of tea. But I don't know if it would prevent me from doing it. Then there's stuff beyond that. For example, I had heard of *A Serbian Film*. I never saw it, but I was really kind of interested in seeing it because it seemed like it was pushing the boundaries. Then as I read more about it I thought, "You know, those are the kind of boundaries I don't really want to push." I learned later that maybe that film was exploitive in some ways. Oddly I decided not to see it and find out.

On the other hand, I saw Gaspar Noé's film, *Irreversible*, which looks like a snuff film for the first 40 minutes, at least until it sort of unfolds and opens up. It's like a thinking man's *Momento*, as the film is told in reverse. When I saw it at TIFF a number of years ago it had arrived after being boo-ed out of

Cannes. And even at the Toronto festival people were walking out of the industry screening in droves. I was on the verge of leaving the screening too, but for some reason I stayed. In the end there was a redemption if one stayed through to the end — and I thought it was really good. If I would have only seen the first 40 minutes and walked out then I probably would have told you it was the worst, most awful, most misguided piece of exploitive bullshit I had even seen. When I saw it through though, the guy changed my point of view and my thinking a little bit. Not necessarily a film I'd recommend to the squeamish among us, but an very interesting lesson in effective storytelling.

So where's that ethical line? I don't know. I mean I wouldn't do something that actually harmed people. It's still movies, this is not defending ourselves against government troops in Aleppo. It's entertainment, and some of it strives towards a cultural relevance and some of it approaches art. But even art, I don't think, can justify things that cause harm. I'm talking about real harm, I'm not talking about hurting somebody's feelings, or provoking people. I'm all over hurting people's feelings, I fucking love hurting people's feelings. Because that's what it's all about. Art and any form of creative expression is about trying to illicit an original response from somebody and make them examine themselves, how they think, what makes them tick, their perceptions of their own reality, all that stuff. Hurting people's feelings comes with the territory but actually hurting people is another thing altogether. And strangely, where that line is can be subjective. Your line, I suppose, would be different than mine.

The only thing that would prevent me from doing something would be an ethical line and I don't know where that line is. I've rendered what some might call extreme violence and I've directed lots of sex scenes, but I've never felt that it was beyond justification. I've always felt comfortable with what it was trying to do, how it was essential to the story or to a character. And I like to think that nobody got hurt in the process, except maybe somebody in the audience's feelings.

What kind of projects do you like to work on? Do they need to challenge you in a specific way or is it the story that drives you?

I think probably more than anything else it's the challenge of the piece that turns my crank. Often it's precisely about how that piece challenges my perception or my ethics, or a judgement I've held about a person or an idea. Generally I'm really drawn to stuff that surprises me.

The question posed in the last thing I did, this miniseries called *Pure* was really about how we can suddenly find ourselves on a very slippery slope after having made a few very minor ethical compromises. What specific set of circumstances have to be present for an insurance salesman to commit murder? Or for an upstanding pillar of the community to steal from the people he purports to help. *Pure* is about a Mennonite pastor forced to work for a Mennonite run cocaine syndicate. He starts out thinking he can take it down from the inside, but he soon has to make so many little ethical and theological compromises.

I've always believed that pretty much any human being is capable of just about anything given the right set of circumstances. We all make decisions based on the here-and-now. As much as we like to run from the here-and-now and stick our faces in our phones and computers, we react in the moment and sometimes do things that we otherwise wouldn't be expected to do.

Maybe it's a more esoteric challenge like, "When do you decide to tell someone that you love deeply that you never want to see them again?" It can be as simple as that and if it's rendered in the right way then it can be very affecting. Those kinds of ethical, moral, and personal challenges are everything that appeals to me in the material I direct.

Would you say a technical challenge plays into it at certain points? For example if you have to shoot something in a way that's never been done before. Do those kinds of challenges appeal to you?

Absolutely they appeal to me. There would have to be something underlying that that is a cinematic or artistic truth or question or challenge, something that needed to be answered or responded to or rendered. Then the actual logistical challenge for me becomes me going into my toolbox and figuring out how I might attack it. I like to think I am equipped to deal with that stuff (at least I hope I am). Of course you have to try to find the wherewithal within the budget constraints and the limitations you have to actually pull it off. That's a challenge that can be fun.

At its core the challenge to me as a director is always 'where's the truth?' Where's the truth in any given scene, where's the truth in any given character, and where's the truth in any given story? The act of rendering that truth as best I can is the challenge. That's far more difficult than trying to figure out how to shoot a battle or how to shoot a car chase, or how to shoot a building being blown up. That shit's easy. Finding the emotional truth of a moment and effectively rendering it is challenging.

Figuring out how to shoot a battle on boats that you can't really control is terrifically enjoyable. Or trying to figure out how to shoot a scene in a set that's four feet by six feet. What do you do? Do you drive yourself nuts and try to punch holes in the walls or do you embrace the set you're in and let that drive the storytelling for that particular scene? All those little mini challenges are part of it too and that's what makes directing so much fun.

Ultimately it's never about the camera tricks or how many crane shots you've got, or some flashy camera move – those things have their place — but for me it's about "what truth is there here?" and "what am I trying to say with this truth?"

What is the most important lesson you've learned as a director?

I would say, "It's learning to talk with my ears." I'm all for having a long discussion with an actor about character over a couple glasses of wine. I could go for hours and hours. At the end of the day it's really about listening, both when an actor is talking to me and when they're performing a scene. Then it is about trying to take it in and understand it, even, and probably most especially, when there's a difference of opinion or when things have gone off message. When I feel the need to go in and shape it or redirect an actor in a specific direction, I've found it's much easier to do so if I've been listening.

Simply learning how to listen was actually a big challenge. I believe ninety percent of directing is listening and watching and being good at both. The noun, "director" implies an outflowing control, and it is partly that. However, to make demands or offer direction without a willing ear or open mind is creatively moronic, in my opinion.

Among my long list of stupid analogies is the notion that human beings, in general, are snowflakes. Actors especially, each one of them is different and each one of them requires a slightly different approach. And sometimes the approach has to be, "No, it's like this!" simple and direct. But sometimes — most of the time — the approach is a lot less direct and a whole lot more open and giving. It does depend on the person. Some people respond to nothing but, "Faster! Slower. Louder! Softer." And I've worked with people like that.

I've worked with a cinematographer where I was like "You know what John, because this is the last time he's here and they both know he's on a suicidal fool's errand, I want this to be really moody. The negative spaces I think can represent the space between the two of them, because I want to know…blah, blah, blah." And his response was, "You want it dark? I'll give you dark." He listened. He understood me even though he spoke a bit of a different emotional language. In spite of my verbal diarrhea, he got it. And so I looked at him and said, "That's exactly it," and he said, "Good, I'm glad."

As a director you are the final arbiter of the way things are going to go. Ultimately it is the director who will decide when to say "Cut, print and move on." And ultimately, that's a decision to say "Okay, that's what this scene's about right now." It's interesting being the biggest ear in the room and probably the smallest mouth, well maybe not the smallest mouth, but it helps to listen more than you talk.

Were there any other challenges you had to overcome?

When you're directing it feels like you're answering ten thousand questions a day. Half the questions you get asked are done in such a way because people want to get the answer they want. It's kind of like writing. I like to think the foundation of writing is the foundation of the human experience, in the sense that people seldom say what they really mean. They almost always say what they think will get them what they want.

In directing on a film set half of the questions will have 'yes' or 'no' answers, and with the other half you'll realize that there's another question behind the question. That's a challenge; trying to understand what an actor means when they do something or what a script means when you read it. Trying to understand what the cinematographer or the props guy or the wardrobe person means when they come up to you and ask you a question like:

"Do you want her wearing a scarf?"

"Well she's going outside, why wouldn't she wear the scarf?"

"Well in the scene after this, which we shot yesterday, she didn't have on the scarf when she went outside."

"Well then why didn't you ask me the question with that information included?"

Have you had role models or mentors that have challenged you over the years?

Most are influences I had earlier in my life that are still present with me today. I look at people who have dedicated their lives to a certain form of expression, but they've been forced to fight for their ability to express themselves. I deeply admire that. I look at an artist like Ai Weiwei who has had to go through so much, and I see the work he does and it's mind-bogglingly complex, accessible, and beautiful, and like a punch in the gut all at once. I just think, "How does he do it?" I count my blessings because for me it's been so easy in comparison.

I admire certain artists of cinema such as Satajit Ray, Akira Kurosawa, Robert Altman, and Francis Coppola for example. I admire certain works as well because not everybody's on their A-game 24/7. Nobody's perfect all the time. I hear people say stuff like "Director so-and-so's worst work is better than almost everybody else's". I don't buy it. The only thing worse than sitting through a bad film is sitting through a bad play.

In terms of TV shows, when you go in to work on a show that has multiple directors, would you say that's a challenge? Stylistically, how do you match it? How does it work?

Well when working as an episodic TV director, that's very true, it's a challenge. You have to respect the paradigm of the show. It also depends if you're coming in just for an episode, which I don't do very much of anymore. A show like *Daredevil* has a very definite approach, a predescribed look if you will, but even within that approach, you can stretch and grow. What I like to think I can do is take their pre-described paradigm and reshape it a little bit. It's kind of a challenge, working within a set of rules where you bend and push the rules and try to improve them, but it's fun.

You rely a little bit more on the cinematographer. And a lot of it has to do with the writing and with the production design. You know you can't go in and shoot six consecutive scenes in a master shot. You have to shoot coverage so they can get the show down to time. You know that it's running 48 minutes and it has to be 44 minutes in the final cut, so how are you going to get it down in time? You have to be able to cut.

So much of what a show is and feels like is determined by the production design and the way it's lit. I haven't been on a lot of shows where they walk in and go, "We don't use anything wider than a 35 and never go tighter than a 200." I've never been on a show like that, but there are limitations when one is among many directors on a series. That doesn't mean those limitations have to stifle creative drive. If anything it sometimes takes a bit more creativity to find your own voice within something that's already somewhat visually and stylistically established.

It was the opposite for me in this mini-series I just did. One part of it takes place in a Mennonite community and the other takes place amongst cops, drug-dealers and the world outside the closed colony of Mennonites. I shot all the cops and drug-dealers with long lenses and dense, messy frames with lots of foreground, and I shot the Mennonites with wide lenses right up in their faces so that their environments were more apparent, more present. I wanted their environment, or their backgrounds to help inform who they were. Now if it was a show where they had a run of directors, I suppose I could come in as an executive producer and say, "Here's the approach," and would tell the cinematographer to feel free to mess with it. I would say, "I really want the environments to inform the Mennonite characters. I want the characters in the outside world to be claustrophobically entrapped in their environments. If you find a better way to do that than what I've described here in my little visual primer then have at it." In the end, the result would be different than the one a single director over multiple episodes could deliver.

Many of the challenges can be posed by the budget too because the style of the show is often governed by that. You look at what David Fincher did with the first season of *House of Cards*. Cameras just sat there in these really hard deliberate compositions and they hardly moved. If they moved, it would be very, very classical and elegant. To me, that's a reaction to cameras on the shoulder. Cameras on the shoulder, shaky-cam, the verité style, can move a set a lot faster than cameras on dollies or cameras on a set of sticks. Many stylistic choices on television shows have to do with budgets and schedules more than style or visual approach.

On *Pure* we had limited budget resources, but I didn't want to go the easy route. I wanted to approach the material classically. Close and wide in the Mennonite world, and busy, dense and compressed outside of it. The long lenses were easy to handle. Long lenses hide a multitude of sins. But wide lenses can feel so much more cinematic at times, especially on television because they're so rarely used. I presented my cinematographer with the challenge of how to shoot close and wide on a low budget television mini-series. I said "Tom, the only way we're going to be able to do this close/wide thing is if I can do this end of the table with a camera in the middle and that end of the table with a camera in the middle at the same time. We have to be able to shoot in two opposite directions at once." And he did it! I really wanted the camera to be in the space between the characters. It just looks different I think, partly because that's something you don't often see in television. The camera is so often outside the space, it's over the shoulder, it's got a long lens. In this case, I wanted it in the space between the characters because I think there's something very cinematic about that. Even when it had to be outside of the space, it was on the edge of the space. I left a whole lot of negative space in the frame.

Those were difficult challenges as a director that I was only able to overcome with the help of a production designer and a cinematographer who were willing to go there with me. I produced a look primer and I said, "Here's what I want to do. How are we going to do this?" And Tom said, "We'll break the kitchen table in half and we'll put the camera in the middle. We're using REDs, they're not going to be that big, we can do it." We did it and it was amazing!

For an episodic TV show, is it more of a challenge for the new director coming in or would you say more of a challenge for the crew and the cast working with the new director?

I think it's a little harder for the new person coming in

because the family's already been there, they've already been having dinner on a weekly basis and all of a sudden you have to come in and act like you know everybody. That's a challenge for sure. When I did jobs for hire like that the first thing was to figure out who the horse's mouth was. It's not always the showrunner, sometimes it's somebody else. I had to find out who is ultimately making decisions because that's the person I needed to be able to be in contact with on a regular basis. Then the next thing you need to do is figure out who you're going to be dealing with on the floor. You're not necessarily going to be speaking the same language as the cinematographer and the production designer, but as long as you're openly communicating, you can usually sort it out with them.

You're going to get information from everybody. The location manager's going to tell you stuff about the political landscape and the production manager or drivers are going to tell you something about it. You really have to figure it out for yourself because everybody's got a dog in the fight and they've all got an agenda. That political stuff is unimaginably fucking annoying and I can't stand it. I'd rather just do the job.

Do you have any tips for aspiring directors when it comes to facing challenges?

You must have gotten into this business because you thought it challenged you in some way and now here you are, have fun. The challenges are part of the fun, and sometimes it's the challenges you don't expect. It's not about how to direct something, or how to direct an actor, or how to make the car chase really cool, or whether or not you're going to storyboard the scene. The bigger challenge may be committing to the notion of the career to the point where you do what's necessary to realize your goal. And that may have nothing to do with directing. It might just be reading as many books and scripts as you can, going to the art gallery as much as you can, taking an improv class, doing a scene study class, or writing a script. All of those things inform you as someone who wants to tell stories. Also listening – if you listen long enough and well enough then situations and people are really easy to manage.

If you're thinking, "I don't want to do all of that, I just want to direct" maybe you've chosen the wrong line of work. If you want to direct then there's a little bit of work you have to do beforehand.

There's the challenge of just being persistent. There's the challenge of just finding the truth. There's the challenge of finding and trying to work on things that are personally and creatively enriching. Then there's the challenge of being in a situation that feels personal to you, where you have something deeply personal to say, and getting over the insecurity of going out and saying it.

At times in the business, the challenge can be being in the moment. The results have become so very important, especially when there's a lot of money behind it and a lot of interested parties breathing down a director's neck. The challenge would be, "Okay, screw the process. What we really have to focus on is the end game and the result." Well you know what? I've been doing this a good while and it didn't take me that long to realize that it's what I live every day.

Even when I'm not shooting I'm still working on stuff that's related to directing. If I can't stop and appreciate the process for what it is and enjoy the people I'm surrounded with for 12 or 13 or 14 hours a day or not enjoy the interactions between myself and my creative colleagues, then why am I doing this?

The process for me is as important as the result. The result is what the result is. You always want it to be great, you want it to be the best thing ever, but when you live it, it's important not to pass it by.

8

COMMUNICATE YOUR VISION

VISION IS A WORD with a lot of weight. It is the only word that accurately summarizes the job of a director. A director without a vision is like an olympic athlete without any training. From my viewpoint it's the only part of the job description that can't really be taught. Either you have vision or you don't. Technical skills and leadership skills can be learned but having a clear and creative vision cannot.

The director's vision is the driving force behind the project. It is what keeps the director focused and on point and it's also what keeps the cast and crew on track. Issues tend to arise when the director does not have a clear vision or when their vision gets distorted or veers off course throughout the production process.

You may be wondering: How do you know if what you are thinking is actually your vision for the project? To put it simply, you will just *know*. If you have a 'vision' but you keep going back and forth on it and it does not feel quite as solid or certain, then you have not figured out the vision.

In this context the definition of vision is referring to the ability to plan future activities using imagination. Vision is essentially a fancy way of saying that you are creating a blueprint for the production. It is what everyone involved is working towards and it is what people look to when they feel stuck.

Vision is aligned with the purpose, and while for some projects the purpose may have been determined by the screenwriter(s), the vision is what comes from the director. In some cases the screenwriter will also direct, but most of the time the director's vision has to align with the purpose of the story or script. No producer ever wants to have to deal with a situation where the screenwriter and the director have creative disagreements because the vision and purpose do not align.

In my viewpoint, it is part of the core of the director's job to communicate his/her vision to everyone involved. Depending on the person or department, this may be done at different stages. In pre-production it is important to communicate the vision to the key department heads including the cinematographer, key grip, production sound mixer, production designer, set decorator, costume designer, and of course the producers. These are the key players who end up managing other people so if they are not clear on the director's vision, they cannot do their jobs properly. The last thing a director wants is for there to be creative clashes between departments which only occurs when the vision was not stated at the very beginning of the process.

> "The hardest part about directing is getting everyone on the same page."
> **- Rob Marshall**

Once production rolls around, it would be wise to have

a crew meeting on the first day to make it known what your vision is and to get everyone on board. This is also a great time to clear up any misunderstandings. Of course it is also crucial to talk to the cast about the vision. Your vision will inform the choices they make as actors so in my mind the more clear they are on the end result before you start production, the easier it is for them to bring their characters to life and ultimately help you tell the story the way you want to.

During post-production the key team members who need to be on the same page about the vision include the post-production supervisor, the editor, the VFX supervisor (assuming visual effects are required), the sound designer, and the composer. You would be prudent to actually tell the post-production team during pre-production because the absolute worst scenario to have to handle would be misunderstandings of the vision during post-production. On the other hand, the vision can evolve throughout the production process – not change direction but instead become more specific. It would be wise to review the vision again at the post-production stage in case you have had small tweaks or inspirations that are important to share.

I always think in post when I'm on set which is why it is so important for me to be super clear on what my vision is. I'm in the moment with the actors during their performances, but I'm always thinking, 'If I cut to one shot and then cut to a different shot, is that going to work well coming together in post?', and 'Will it play out the way I see it in my vision?' While I do plan the shots ahead of time, things can change or be adjusted on the actual shoot date, so you need to be prepared to make changes on the spot.

It's almost like you have to constantly run through the final cut in your mind as you're shooting and thinking of it as an audience member in post-production so that you are actively asking yourself, 'Will I be pulled out of the story?' If the answer is 'no' then move to the next shot, but if there is a slight chance that it might be jarring for the audience, you should shoot it until it is the way it needs to be. To give an example, while filming *Dinner With Bernice*, I wanted to get a point of view (POV) shot of the main character, Gwen, standing over her neighbour's dead body. We got the shot, but we were racing against the light and had to move on and I hadn't gotten an over-the-shoulder shot of her looking down at the body which was crucial to show the perspective of where she was standing in the room. My DP assured me that we would be able to flip the POV shot in post-production to get the desired effect, so I trusted his judgement. I still had my concerns that it might not work the way we intended. Flipping the shot in post worked, but had it not, the audience may have been pulled out the the story.

To sum it up there are three reasons as to why it is super important to communicate your vision:

1. To provide the team with a blueprint and with a specific purpose.

2. To keep the team focused and working towards the same end result.

3. To clear up misunderstandings and eliminate the possibility of creative head-butting.

Now that we have discussed what vision is, why it is important to communicate it and to whom to communicate it, it is time to go through *how* to communicate it.

At the end of the day you can communicate it however you like, but here are some suggestions to make sure that you don't run the risk of there being any misunderstandings. Misunderstandings are the first step to creative disagreements between you and the departments, and you definitely do *not* want that.

To make this easier I will use a production analogy. Let's break up the strategy into three sections: pre-communication, communication, and post-communication. Each section will provide strategies you can use to help you ensure that you impart your vision clearly, as well as some helpful tips.

PRE-COMMUNICATION

This is the preparation you do before even opening your mouth to disseminate your vision.

All the work you do normally as a director including the storyboards, ideas for costumes, character vision boards, ideal locations, etc., is part of the preparation, but putting together all of those things only provides you with the pieces of the vision, it doesn't actually allow you to articulate it in a couple of sentences.

Use these steps as a means of writing out your vision as what you would ideally communicate to every crew member and every actor on the team.

Step 1: Do all of the creative prep work you would do for the project (i.e.: shot lists, etc., – see list above).

Step 2: Take a look at all the elements and find key words or phrases that apply to everything. More often than not these words will be feelings, moods or tones, character arcs, or themes. Write the key words down.

Step 3: Take the key words and phrases and rewrite them again in list form and in an order that makes logical sense to you. The order and length will depend on the project, but as a rule of thumb this list should be one page or less.

Step 4: Look at the list you wrote in Step 3 and no matter the length, make everything even more concise and clear. Rewrite the list as two or three sentences that describe the end result you are aiming for. This is your vision.

Step 5: Read the updated list from Step 4 out loud to yourself. While this may seem like a useless silly step, speaking the vision you wrote out loud does two things: it makes it more real to you, and it allows you to spot discrepancies and parts that are unclear.

Step 6: Read the same updated list from Step 4 out loud to somebody else (ideally not someone on the crew or cast) and ask them if they understood it. Ask them if they think any details are missing. The reason you read it to someone not on the production team or cast is because if someone unfamiliar with the project can understand the vision then you are golden.

The tricky thing with communicating your vision is that it's easy to make it convoluted and detailed, it is a challenge to keep it concise and tell people in a way that is simple to understand.

COMMUNICATION

The most effective way to communicate your vision is to take the list that you came up with from the previous steps and say it out loud to all those involved. Now, the above steps are to communicate your vision in a general way. It would be advised to go back and create a more specific vision for each department as well. Your overall vision is made up of a bunch of smaller visions for the finished project. If you're like me and see the pictures you want in the final edit in your mind when you're first creating the ideas, then this would be a great step. You want to make it more specific because the parts of the vision that apply to the costume department won't necessarily also apply to the sound department.

Follow the same steps, but only use the elements pertinent to each specific department. That combined with the overall vision will give every person involved in making your vision a reality an aligned purpose and clearly stated goal.

POST-COMMUNICATION

After your vision has been communicated you should ask questions (to your key people at the very least) to make sure that everyone understands. It's easy to ask "Does that make sense?" or "Is that clear to everyone?", but sometimes people are uncomfortable stating it if they aren't following what you're saying or aren't sure of a detail.

Another way to approach it would be to ask them to repeat the vision back. This can be done verbally or they can write it down and get you to check it. To some this sounds like an exercise a teacher would give students, but the last thing you want is for people to move ahead based on a misunderstood vision and then create problems for the production later on. Get them to fully understand it then they can move ahead successfully.

When you communicate your overall vision to the cast and crew you can get them to repeat it back to you at the same time, that way no one is being called out to do it in front of the entire group.

CHALLENGES WHEN THE VISION IS NOT COMMUNICATED PROPERLY

I will be frank and say that these tips and strategies are ones that I have only recently discovered to be the correct way of doing things. I have made mistakes in the past of not communicating my vision as clearly as I could have and it created frustrations on set. Most of the frustration was on my end though, but looking back I know that I was really just frustrated with myself for not communicating my vision more clearly.

I suppose I've been lucky that I've been able to work with cast and crew who just get it. I didn't have to say much for them to understand what my vision was. Of course hindsight is 20/20, so looking back on pretty much every project I've ever worked on, there are dozens of ways I could have communicated better. I'm happy that I now have the tools and strategies that I can use moving forward which is why I wanted to share them with you in this book.

One example where I could have done better at explaining my vision was on the test shoot for *Revolution 10*. It was a small shoot with only a handful of crew members and the lead actors. I did all my preparation and wrote down all of the shots, but on the day of the shoot there were some miscommunications between myself and the cinematographer. There was a disconnect in understanding the shots I wanted for one of the setups and there was the rush of figuring the logistics of where cameras should be because I did not plan it out enough ahead of time. When I clarified and more clearly explained what was in my head using images and symbols drawn out on paper the cinematographer understood what I was seeing in my head and the process of setting up the shot became simple.

It was frustrating and difficult for the cinematographer to figure out how to deliver what I wanted. But what did I expect? I did not give him what he needed ahead of time so we were forced to whip it out quickly on the day of. I was glad that once the shots were clarified the shoot ran very smoothly, but my mistake put us back about an hour and forced us to shoot later than expected. I take full responsibility for the miscommunications and confusion that day. I am also fully aware that I should have planned better and had a meeting with the cinematographer ahead of time to discuss all the shots in detail instead of leaving most of that to the morning of the shoot. Part of the issue was that I thought of it as only a test shoot and not a normal shoot like every other one.

> "People think that the directors direct actors. No. Really, what the director's doing is directing the audience's eye through the film."
> **- Julianne Moore**

I am thankful I had that experience despite some of the setbacks because it taught me a lot about the logistics in producing live-action interactive stories, which was the ultimate purpose of the test shoot. In the end it was a great learning experience on many levels. I now make sure to meet with cinematographers at least twice during pre-production to hash out the creative and technical details. Of course the larger the scope of the project the more meetings are required.

I have been fortunate in that I have not had many challenges when communicating my vision and creative ideas to cast or crew. I tend to work with people who have a bit of a gift in reading my mind. That has just as much to do with my ability to communicate as to the listening and implementation skills of the crew and cast that I work with.

I have had times where I did not clarify some technical aspects of my vision. For example, I have produced and directed shoots where I have worked with non-cinematographers as camera operators and I have made the mistake of not double checking the settings on the cameras they were operating. As a result some footage turned out slightly grainy or overexposed. Similar to the previous situation, I take full responsibility for the results.

Most times it is the small details that can make a huge difference in getting the desired outcome and meeting the technical and creative expectations of the vision. It is a learning curve and the beauty about directing is that as long as your vision is clear in your mind, all you need to ensure is that it is communicated clearly to others. The worst situation you can be in is if *you* are not clear on your own vision because that creates frustration with the people you work with, it creates time lags in production, and it can cause problems in the editing room. A director's vision can truly make or break the final picture.

The best success tip I can provide here is to write down everything. I cannot express enough how writing things down can strip away the fog and make the vision crystal clear. If someone doesn't understand something you are explaining about your vision, draw it out for them or literally spell it out for them.

When deciding on whether to shoot widescreen for a short film called *A Last Wish*, I kept going back and forth in my mind about what I wanted. We were shooting on the RED Scarlet Dragon which provides some good options. We were on site for our first day of principal photography and I still hadn't made a decision. I regret not having done more research on the topic ahead of time, but I couldn't dwell in the past. We had to push forward as we had limited time in that location. The format of the film is an important choice and it had to be made, so I just made the call to shoot in widescreen. It was only when I made a decision that the cinematographer was able to move ahead and set up the shots. If I were to give advice to myself, it would be to not leave big decisions, like finalizing the aspect ratio, to the last minute. I was clearly delaying making a decision because I wasn't sure of that particular element of my vision for the film, and as a result I created a problem for myself on the first day of shooting. What can I say, I'm still learning too.

The bottom line is that if you cannot explain your vision simply then you really don't know what your vision is. When you don't know what your vision is or are wavering on elements of your vision, sometimes the only thing you can do is just decide on something and go with it. Any decision is better than no decision.

INTERVIEW WITH
YANNICK BISSON

Murdoch Mysteries

How would you define 'vision'?

Lots of people talk about vision. To me it's the visual direction that a storyteller wants to impart. The important thing however is that it will only be as good, or I should say as comprehensive, as their ability to communicate it to their team long before the audience.

Why do you think it is important for a director to communicate his/her vision?

Once a director has begun to lay out the pieces that he or she requires to tell the story effectively, there's an army of creative people ready to build on and add to the narrative as a whole. Without this clear communication your crew is without a rudder and unable to lay out the countless contributions (and alternate ideas for unforeseen circumstances) you could have at your disposal.

Do you do anything in preparation before communicating your vision to the key crew and cast? If so, what do you do?

One of the tools I use is a simple phone camera and a stand-in. I take pictures of the "characters" in the actual locations, from the intended points of view. I then stitch them together with footnotes in a program called Evernote. This is by no means complex or final, but it creates a sort of storyboard that all departments can work off of and use to get clarity. This is particularly helpful for action sequences with multiple screen directions and axes.

To whom do you communicate your vision and why?

Showbiz is really driven by money...or lack of it! There isn't a soul on set that isn't required. This means everyone is needed and there to preform a given task. It's important that everyone knows what's happening. Directors often assume that everyone knows what's going on at all times (They should! But...). Delegation of communication is often handled by the assistant director department, but in the moment the final touches must be reiterated by the director. He or she can't simply bark from a chair a mile away.

In your opinion and experience, what is the most effective way to communicate the vision?

Most people can understand or relate to a "feeling". Whether it's sadness, fear, anxiety or joy, people can get the general idea of emotional context. I usually start with that. The actors work well from this point. Then the technical points to capture this feeling get laid out. This could mean anything from a lighting mood to the speed at which the camera operator pans the camera.

What kind of challenges have you encountered when sharing your creative vision and ideas with crew and/or cast? How did you go about overcoming these challenges?

One particular shot in season four of *Murdoch Mysteries* just wasn't coming together for me. It had many moving pieces. The scene was about William seeing his love Julia for the first time in many months. She was now working in a Buffalo children's hospital and the shot was meant to be William's point of view of her and her beauty, as she is revealed amongst all the chaos. There had to be many moving parts; the dozen extras, the camera dolly pushing in etc. The shot was just boring.

I had consciously chosen flowers as a continuing visual theme in the episode so I told all involved that I wanted the sense of a flower blossoming, opening to the sun and radiating beauty at the final image. That did it. The bustle of the hospital graciously parted way for the the leading lady to be revealed with happiness and love in her eyes. Bingo.

Have you had an experience where you didn't communicate your vision in a way that allowed for the intended results? If so, what happened?

I once took for granted that a couple of actors understood a certain aspect of the context that they were meant to convey within an episode. We were pressed for time at the end of the day and the actor was resisting what I was asking him to do. It didn't fit with his understanding of the character. We ran out of time and the piece I was after was lost. Later in conversation I asked what the issue was and it simply was a lack

165

of communication on my part. A tiny thing, but it could have paid big dividends.

Do you have any success tips for aspiring directors about relaying their creative vision to their team?

Just like anything in life, most of us can only retain so much information in one bite. I try to keep this in mind at all times. When directing actors (I've been acting for over 30 and have worked with hundreds of directors) it's important to not overwhelm them with useless crap that only a robot could process. One or two notes, at the most 3, between takes is all that's needed. If you still need to tweak a performance, do another take. The same applies to all the technicians you work with. Everyone is truly trying to do their best, don't put them off!

9

COLLABORATE AND LISTEN

COLLABORATION WITH CAST AND crew is part of the job as a director because everyone involved in the production must work as a team in order to accomplish goals.

One key action I take on every shoot no matter how small or how large, nor how short or long, is to create introductions for the crew and cast who do not know each other. Making sure that the crew and cast know one another's names is key, not just for the morale of the group, but for communication's sake. It makes a big difference when crew members address one another by first name instead of "hey you!" or nothing at all.

There is a cycle. Communication leads to collaboration, and collaboration leads to a result being produced. Have you ever seen a productive set where everyone is woking independently and there is zero collaboration? No. Never, because it would be impossible to produce anything of value and quality without a team of people working towards a common goal.

By establishing a policy of openness and an environment of no judgement or better yet of understanding, a director can go from being a visionary to a legendary leader. The essence of understanding is communication. Listening is a key part of that puzzle. Sometimes it means that you need to listen to cast or crew one-on-one when there is an issue to handle, but sometimes it means listening to what people are really saying when they talk. That does not mean you need to learn mind-reading tricks. It means that if you learn how to understand people and how they behave, you can listen to them without them saying one word. It is about reading the person and the situation using your instinct, mixed with a bit of logic. Depending on the situation at hand it may not be appropriate to act on that instinct. It is more effective and less invasive to let people come to you when they are ready to talk about something, though it doesn't hurt to check in with someone privately if you have a concern as it would allow an opening for a conversation where they can feel comfortable to talk.

> "To direct actors is difficult. To direct actors in another language is more difficult, but directing non-actors in another language is one of the craziest things that I have done and one of the most rewarding experiences I have had."
> **- Alejandro Gonzalez Inarritu**

At the end of the day being an approachable director means that you are working as a collaborator and you are taking the time to listen to the people who help make your vision come to life. Now on the other hand there is a fine line between being approachable and collaborative and being everyone's friend and a wishy-washy, indecisive leader.

I have heard that women tend to be more collaborative and listen well by nature which is great, but a director cannot let that detract her from being decisive. She should be someone who can confidently say 'no' to an idea, and who can quite literally direct any problems that she doesn't have time to handle to a producer or another leader on set.

I may sound a bit contradictory here because I'm saying that sometimes to be a good leader, you have to say 'no' and let other people handle issues, but that's exactly it. It is part of being a good leader; knowing when to step in and when to pass an issue over to a producer to handle. I will say that if there is ever a problem with a person (cast or crew) who works directly with you on a daily basis, it would be prudent that you are the one to confront the issue. It might be helpful to get a producer involved for some assistance especially if the issue is more major than just a small miscommunication.

Let's get into the topic of collaboration a bit more. As mentioned at the beginning of the chapter, communication leads to collaboration, but that can't be accomplished unless people get to know their colleagues better.

There are a handful of great exercises that I have learned over the years and know to be effective in building a better working environment. Some are super quick and some can be done over a short period of time. Below are my top 3 exercises.

EXERCISE #1: NAME MEMORY GAME

This one is a great exercise to get at least ten people to know one another's names within a few minutes. Stand in a circle. One person starts and says their name. The person to their right then says the first person's name then their own name. The third person, or the person to the right of the second person, says the first person's name, the second person's name, then their own name. And so on and so forth until you get to the last person, standing to the left of the first person. The last person has the toughest job which is to say everyone's name in order. Since this is a memory game and you want it to be a quick exercise, it is best to do in smaller groups of 8-12 people especially if you are doing this on the first day of filming with the entire crew. This game definitely tests one's listening abilities because if someone is listening properly, they don't need to memorize all the names.

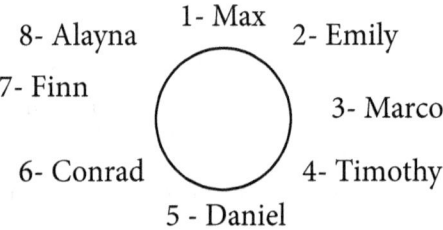

EXERCISE #2: HEY, I KNOW YOU!

Since the first exercise is only really feasible on smaller sets, this next one is one that can work on a massive big budget film with hundreds of people. It's more of a get-to-know-you over the course of the first week of production. Get everyone to write their name on a name tag or create something crafty, like a headdress or a bandana that has their name on it. As the shoot goes on, everyone talks to one another and gets to know one another. The goal by the end of the week is for each person to get to know five people and learn three interesting things about them. Each person has to write down those three things and the name of the person whose qualities they belong to, then read them to a second person. Not only does this exercise get everyone talking, but it gets people to actually learn things about each other. The only way for people to succeed at this exercise is to listen intently to the people they meet. To make it more of a challenge, do not write down the three things you learn about each person. After all, you don't really do that in real life when you meet new people.

EXERCISE #3: HAPPY HELPER

To encourage collaboration in the work environment in every stage of production this is a great exercise. This game is quick and simple. Every person has to do two simple tasks on a daily basis. The first is to help someone else with something they are struggling with or just to lighten their load. The second is to tell one person something that they have done well and validate their good work. The end result of people actually putting this exercise into practice is a highly positive and motivated crew with a willingness to help others and validate good behaviour and work. The bigger end result is a successful set full of happy people.

To say that there is one way to get the entire production team working as a positive cohesive force would be a lie. There are many ways to go about creating that, but there is only one thing that a director should put attention on and that is all the good things. I am sure you have heard that 'you get what you put your attention on' or some derivation of that, but it is the truth.

If as a leader all you are thinking about are the problems,

both technical and interpersonal, you'll only create more problems. It is not to say that you shouldn't handle problems as they present themselves, but it becomes a delicate balance of handling issues that actually have an impact on the success of the group and the project versus handling issues just for the sake of feeling like you did something productive. You can always ask a producer or someone you trust to handle the smaller problems if need be.

You are the leader and your judgement calls on every level dictate the result and the success of your vision. You have to take responsibility for your choices, even if they are the wrong ones, but trust me when I say that you are better off creating a positive, understanding, and collaborative set.

Collaboration manifests itself from two or more people working together to create something. The most important part of this process is making decisions. It can depend on the project, but on most occasions it is good to have the key members of the crew a part of your decision-making process from the early stages.

Working closely with the key department heads and brainstorming the best ways to accomplish things is the best way to make sure that your project goes off without a hitch. Often times certain decisions are made for you and the department heads in the script, but anything that is not specified in the script can technically be left up to interpretation by the director. If the vision is clear then involving other members of the executive team is the best thing you can do to ensure the ultimate success for the project. Film has a lot of moving parts and you want them all working cohesively together rather than against one another.

I've had an interesting experience creating and developing *Revolution 10* where being collaborative and listening were applicable skills from the get go. The process took over two years and it was a tedious yet exhilarating process. Development could be argued to be the first stage of a vision. It all starts with an idea and, slowly but surely, and through hours and hours of brainstorming notes and red scribbles, it turns into a screenplay. Developing this particular project put me in a particularly fascinating position. Knowing that I would be directing the film, I almost was able to work backwards, or rather to move backwards and forwards in time in my head, from development to the fine cut to production and back to development.

The development sessions I had with the screenwriter, Sonja, were some of the most riveting and exhausting ones I've ever had. It was the first time that either have us had ever developed an interactive feature from the first skeleton to a flushed out storyline so we had to collaborate and listen to one another's ideas. I was so lucky to find a development and writing partner that I work so well with because we spent a lot of time together and had to bounce off each other in an open and critical way. I find that writers who brainstorm well also think critically and always make the best choice for the story. Personal pride never comes into play and being a good listener plays a big part in that. Our collaboration allowed for so much magic to happen because when I would give direction from the viewpoint of production, or from the viewpoint of the editing room, she would take that direction and decide if it worked from her viewpoint as the screenwriter. Over time we found a good rhythm and we figured out what strategies of our collaboration benefited us and the story the most and we kept doing what worked.

I discovered that working as a director on set is very different from working as a director in development, but the two can move together like waves in the ocean. The vision was connected from the inception of the idea to the completion of the script. The one thing that helped keep me grounded throughout that process was my confidence in making decisions, and trusting that those decisions would bring the story to life in the screenplay — and it did. The moral of the story is that collaboration and listening skills are assets when you are working on projects from the early stages all the way through to distribution.

In general, I want to listen to the advice of the cinematographer and the lead actors. The visuals and the on screen performances tied in with my directing style and leadership abilities are at the core of making a project successful. While all other key elements including production design, sound design and costume design also add value to a production, the cinematography and the performances dance together, and when choreographed by the director, can either make or break a story.

I love letting actors play around and make different choices. Unless I have a very specific note or piece of direction, I like seeing what the actors bring to the table. Actors are artists and visionaries in their own right and as directors we have to treat them as such. They are not puppets or parrots who can be placed in one position and told how to speak. My guiding factor is if the notes I give help nudge them in the right direction and get them closer to how I envision the story, and improve their performances, then I've done my job. The danger is that if you lose touch with what you see in your mind then you can stop caring about the performances and become complacent. That is a dangerous place to be in as a director since your vision is the initial spark that breathes life into a story.

Collaborating with actors and getting them to understand which of the pivotal parts of their character's journey are the most impactful on the overall vision can bring actors from just repeating the dialogue to embodying it. Your story has to be living and breathing. The ebbs and flows of the story are what make it compelling so when an actor listens to your direction and applies it, and when you collaborate and allow them to make insightful choices that benefit the story, you will see amazing results. My advice would be to actively find moments during every stage of a production to collaborate and exchange ideas with your team.

> "I love directing scenes that I'm not in because suddenly I really feel like a filmmaker which is a different thing."
> **- Lena Dunham**

All creative ventures have more than one creative person involved. As the director you have to walk the line of collaboration and decisiveness. You have to lose the egotism when you're fighting for a creative idea that doesn't serve the vision. At the same time you need to be vigilant about making sure that any decisions about any part of the project, from set design to sound effects, are aligned with your vision.

Create a work environment where collaborating and listening to the people around you is your status quo, although that doesn't mean all the ideas should be included.

As the leader you have to tell the cast and crew that you will do your best to take the time to hear suggestions and solutions, but will not make promises you can't keep. You have to show others that you have respect for their talents and that you are grateful for their commitment to achieving the desired end result.

"Collaborate and listen" are not just silly words of encouragement we hear as kids, they are truths that lay the foundation for healthy, strong bonds, and ultimately allow us as directors to create beautiful masterpieces.

INTERVIEW WITH
PAUL GROSS

Men With Brooms, Passchendaele,
Hyena Road

How do you ensure that your entire production team is working well together?

I've found there is no substitute for talking everything through with each department, at length, in detail and repeatedly. In the case of *Passchendaele*, I created an extensive document, including drawings of blocking and, when useful, photographs from the period, excerpts for writing about the period — anything that could give the creative team a starting point in terms of what we were collectively trying to achieve. With *Hyena Road* it was a similar process except that instead of historical records, I had actual veterans from the conflict in Afghanistan as well as a sixty hours of raw footage I'd shot while in the war zone which we could use for reference. The challenge with *Hyena* is that we had very little time to shoot a very ambitious film so I spent an enormous amount of time with Arv Greywal (Production Designer) and Karim Hussain (Director of Photography) working out how to accomplish this. Sometimes together, sometimes just one on one. We took about a year to prepare for the film and used the time to bring any and all ideas forward, narrowing down to those that were the best and most effective.

The key thing is that everyone has to know where we're headed and what the film is trying to capture — whether that's a tone, an idea, an emotion etc. As a director, you are the keeper of the heartbeat of the film, but this does not mean that you know everything. You assemble a group of people around you who are vastly more skilled at what they do than you could ever hope to be, hurl a series of challenges at them and extend to them creative ownership of the endeavour. By this, I mean, they have to understand it is as much their movie as it is yours and that their ideas — exceptional or ridiculous — are all welcome. This is not lip service, at least not for me. Long ago, as an actor and a writer, I learned that the project will only be as good as those gathered with you to create it and those artists will only be at their best when you not only expect it of them but welcome it.

In short, making sure that collaboration succeeds is largely an exercise in losing your own ego.

In what capacity do you involve other members of the executive team in your decision making?

This is kind of similar to the previous question, but I involve everyone in the team to the fullest extent that I can and welcome comments from everyone in the production even if they are about things not strictly in their department. In my experience, everyone in a film thinks deeply about the project and is committed to it utterly and to ignore or exclude their contributions would expose you to missing out on a vitally important contribution someone might make. That being said, it's anything but a free for all. Someone has to make decisions and that someone is the director. I try to set the course, in essence saying this is where we have to end up. Everyone throws in their ideas, their notions of how to arrive there. It's up to the director to choose those suggestions that will most efficiently and effectively get us there.

Do you see any benefits of collaborating with other directors or producers on a project? If so, what are they?

I don't talk much with other directors about a project, unless it's over a technical matter like how to work achieve a certain shot, for example. I do however, talk a lot with producers. In my case, I've worked twice with Niv Fichman and our collaboration is spectacular. He's got a tremendous eye and great taste, and his thoughts about casting, script, the edit etc., are always invaluable. He is as much a part of the creative team as anyone else and I'm fortunate to enjoy that creative partnership.

What has been your best experience on a production where you felt the production team worked well together?

I think both *Passchendaele* and *Hyena Road* were exceptional experiences in terms of the production team gelling and contributing and going that extra ten feet that takes an idea from being good to being shockingly good. Both productions had huge challenges physically and the shoots were demanding and tough. Without that sense of collective collaboration and collective purpose they would have been impossible to pull off.

Whose advice do you tend to listen to most during a production and why?

I listen to everyone really, but I suppose when you're actually shooting the movie I listen to the DP and the First AD the most. The DP because he/she is the one moving through the shot list with me and if we're running into trouble with time or light I need to know what we can do to compensate. Equally, the First AD is the person with an eye on the pulse of the set and how the day is actually unfolding as opposed to how we might have wished it to unfold. I find that constantly checking in with them usually means I can stay on top of the day and accomplish everything we set out to accomplish.

How do you collaborate and work with actors on set?

I am an actor so I like to think my relationship with actors is pretty good. I know roughly what they need and how to provide them with it. More importantly, I respect the intuitive knowledge good actors all possess. They have an instinct for bullshit whether it's in the blocking of a scene or a hiccup in the writing. And when an actor stumbles on something or hits a snag I immediately know there's something wrong with what we're doing and will adjust. In some respects, actors are a little like Formula 1 race car drivers. You have this huge team that builds a complex machine and then you need the driver, the person with the courage and madness to take that machine right up to the breaking point. If there is something wrong, they will know and you ignore them at your peril.

Was there an experience when you were starting out as a director that allowed you to recognize the importance of collaboration and listening?

I learned the importance of it as an actor and on a couple of projects where the directors not only seemed to have no interest in what the actors were thinking, but actively resented them. It was strangely self-destructive and the projects suffered because of it. As I gained in experience I realized the attention one needs to pay to actors must equally be paid to everyone else on the creative team. When I started directing it wasn't a lesson to be learned so much as applied.

Any other comments or stories that you would like to add?

Film is a ludicrously complex art form, one that has hundreds of moving parts and if any number of those moving parts goes awry the entire enterprise will fail. To imagine that any one person can master all of these technical aspects is ridiculous. The great directors, the ones I most admire, are those people who hold in their hearts and minds the soul of the story and can recognize those ideas that will bring that story forward. The most important thing in being the guardian of the story's soul is that the director must need to tell this story with every fiber in her/his being. It is that passion that will galvanize others to follow you and there is no substitute for it. In the words of Werner Herzog, one of the most visionary of filmmakers: "I would travel down to Hell and wrestle a film away from the devil if it was necessary."

10

MOTIVATE AND INSPIRE

I WANTED TO END this book on a topic that not only is one of the most important tasks for a leader, but is also the end goal of any artistic endeavour. As storytellers we want to motivate and inspire audiences, but we also want to motivate and inspire the people working with us.

Before we go any further I think it is important to define what each of those words mean.

Motivate means to push someone you care about to know that they can. The New Oxford American Dictionary defines it as a stimulation of someone's enthusiasm for doing something.

One means of creating motivation is to give constant encouragement by validating improvements of the cast and crew. We all want validation in everything that we do, and when we get it, it motivates us to continue moving forward. It also allows us to get out of the bad habit of looking back on our mistakes. I first learned this golden piece of knowledge working at a summer arts camp. I'd see kids change for the better simply because I gave them enough positive validation to nudge them in the right direction. They grew as people and as young artists and performers.

To inspire means to provide someone with a push towards a state of creation. Usually when one feels inspired they create things or have ideas, and in most cases you don't inspire someone intentionally. It isn't planned. It happens at different times depending on the person. The very least I can do as the director is to do whatever I can to be a great leader and hope that by doing so I can inspire the people I work with to also be leaders. In an ideal scenario the work I direct would hopefully inspire audiences to be the best people they can be, help others, and make the world a better place.

Motivation and inspiration go hand-in-hand. People who inspire and motivate are often also role models to others. They are the kind of people whose actions others want to imitate.

There are a lot of people who I view as role models and who I look to for inspiration. As a director I admire the work of many incredible directors such as George Lucas, Steven Spielberg, Baz Luhrmann, Alfred Hitchcock, John Sturges, Woody Allen, and Richard Donner — *The Goonies* is one of my favourite movies of all time. I respect and enjoy the films they have made and can only assume that their leadership inspired those that have worked with them over the years. The stories they told made me fall in love with film. I find the fact that George Lucas was so young when he made the first *Star Wars* movie extremely inspiring. It proves that when it comes to directing, age is truly just a number.

As an aside, I do find it a bit disappointing that I cannot

name any female directors whose films have truly had a deep seeded impact on me because the sad truth is that most female directors are still not given enough opportunity to tell those stories. Aside from the fact that I do not enjoy saying 'female' director, I do hope that in the next decade I'll be able to add five women to my list of inspiring directors. A few whose past work I have enjoyed include Sofia Coppola, Anne Fletcher, and Penny Marshall. Can I just say that Patty Jenkins taking on a beast like *Wonder Woman* is awesome!

As a producer I admire Christina Jennings because she as built a very successful company by staying true to who she is and working every day to accomplish her goals. She is a brilliant and resilient businesswoman and a shining example to every young producer of how to push the boundaries of storytelling.

Inspirational people in my life include my family and my partner in life, because they always support me in my dreams and goals. When I make my family proud, especially my parents, it gives me a calming sense of accomplishment. Their encouragement and validation of my abilities are what motivate me to push further.

My friends and colleagues that I work closely with are also are a huge source of inspiration for me. When I work and collaborate with people whose presence lifts me up, I push myself harder. I have learned from bad experiences that it is more enjoyable and actually more beneficial from a mental health point of view to surround myself with people who make me want to smile and feel good. People who pull you down and don't care about you are not the people you want to be friends with, and especially not the people you want to work with.

I gravitate towards working with people who are self-motivated and who can also get motivation from working closely with me and the other team members. There are a few things that one can do and say to provide motivation.

For example, when you need another take from the performers in the scene, but they are tired or feel like a bit of a broken record, ask them to run the scene in a completely ridiculous way (like in gibberish or standing on one leg). Assuming there is time in the schedule for this, it will get across to get actors to stop thinking so much and just have fun with it. The next take will have more energy and the actors will feel more motivated overall.

If the crew is moving more slow towards the end of a long day, they probably need a boost. There are two ways you could go about it. You can ask them to take thirty seconds to a minute and jump up and down and shake it out, which will get the blood flowing, or you can ask them to do a short breathing exercise to get back in the present moment. More often than not there is a simple way to motivate the people you work with. Sometimes it is as easy as telling people when they are doing a great job, and if they are feeling frustrated or tired, push them to do more than they thought they could handle. Being a leader means getting people to go out of their comfort zones and pushing them to reach heights they never believed to be possible.

> "Pick up a camera. Shoot something. No matter how small, no matter how cheesy, no matter whether your friends and your sister star in it. Put your name on it as director. Now you're a director. Everything after that you're just negotiating your budget and your fee."
> **- James Cameron**

Encourage them to hustle and they will bring the results if they have a strong enough purpose for being there.

While it is important for a director to be a source of motivation for the cast and crew, it is just as important for the director to be motivated by them. It is a professional relationship built on the idea of exchange. Different people will be inspired by others in different ways. I get a boost from those around me when I see they are enjoying themselves and are making an effort to be helpful. I watch the people I work with and get excited by their energy and willingness to do what is needed to make it the best project it can be.

I also feel really moved when I see actors or crew accomplish something after thinking that they couldn't. That inspires me to push forward. You have to figure out what motivates and inspires you, and more often than not this discovery will be ongoing and will only come from actually doing and creating visual stories. Go out and direct as much as you can. Start with one minute digital shorts and see what happens!

I have found that motivation and inspiration both start with an idea. If I'm trying to get cast and crew on board for a project, it is much easier if they know what the purpose of the project is. If at the very least they are intrigued by it and want to be a part of that journey then I am inclined to have them join the team. There is no exception to this even with people who I have worked with before in the past and who I love and respect and trust dearly. It comes down to whether someone shows enthusiasm for the work from the get-go. I know when an actor is super excited about a role because their reaction to the opportunity is telling. I know when a cinematographer or writer is fired up about working on a project because their eyes light up when they talk about it and you hear a sort of higher tone in their voice.

I have found that pushing myself and any close writing partners that I work with to pump out content and ideas on a frequent basis and at a high speed allows for projects to be opened up to amazing opportunities. The choice to be motivating leader brings positive results. It makes me happy when I can inspire others to do their best and be their best.

In the end your success as a director will come down to you applying all the leadership skills outlined in this book, but your true happiness as a director and as a human being will come when you inspire and motivate those around you. When you are working with a group of people who look to you as their leader, your decisions and the way you carry yourself will have a profound influence on how happy and successful you are as a working director.

I feel it fitting to end this chapter by referring to my favourite quotes. It's tough to choose just one so I will mention two quotes that have the same message.

The first is something that Henry Ford said which was:

**"Whether you think you can or you can't,
either way you are right."**

You have control over what you think you can or cannot do, whether you'd like to believe it or not. We tend to put mental and physical limitations on ourselves, and for what? A dear friend and mentor of mine, Meir Ezra, always says that we have way more potential than we have results to show for it. This applies to life and the business of directing. He's right! Directing anything is a huge job that comes with a ton of responsibility, and rather than buckling under pressure, we have to rise to the occasion and push ourselves harder than we ever have. At least that's the way I see it. With every project I choose to direct, I always try to challenge myself and push myself to do more than I ever thought I could. The funny thing is that I always prove to myself that I can.

The other quote is one that is hard to forget because it tells the truth about how this universe works. It's a quote by Mahatma Ghandi which says:

> "Your beliefs become your thoughts,
> Your thoughts become your words,
> Your words become your actions,
> Your actions become your habits,
> Your habits become your values,
> Your values become your destiny."

I love this quote because it tells the truth about how a person creates their own life. You can apply this to any part of your life, but for directing here's how I see it.

If you believe that being a good director means being a good leader, then your thoughts will be about the management side of things just as much as it is about the technical and creative side of things. If your thoughts also encompass ways to be a great leader on set then the words that you use with the cast and crew will be more positive and encouraging. By using supportive words, even if it is constructive feedback, your actions will be executed in a controlled and calming fashion. It's easy to get frustrated and anxious in a high stress environment like being on a production - yes it's fun, but it's also stressful for a director who has to be thinking about a million things at the same time. If you behave a certain way enough, it will become habitual so that every set you walk onto, no matter who you're working with and whether you like the people you work with or not, your behaviour will be consistent. By making leadership a habit you value the meaning of the word and so whenever you start to stray from being anything other than a leader, it's very obvious to you and those around you. Making leadership one of your values will only solidify your destiny of being a great director.

> "If you just love movies enough, you can make a good one."
> **- Quentin Tarantino**

There are a lot of creative directors with amazing vision, but there are only a handful who are also wonderful leaders. Being a leader can be challenging and messy, but it is much more rewarding when you know that your leadership allowed others to succeed. The rewards are well worth the little bit of discomfort that you may experience when making decisions in a leadership role.

To get through any of the harder times you have to ask yourself on a daily basis: "How badly do you want it?" When you remind yourself that you are directing for a reason, it makes all the not so fun bits of being a leader seem less daunting or scary.

Your passion for the craft is what allows you to tough out the hard times and to inspire you when you need to jump out of the box. Passion is what will fuel you to want to constantly improve.

When people tell me that I inspire them it is the best compliment I could get. It means that I'm doing my job and that I'm doing it well. Performers respect me as a director because I respect their talents and the contributions they make to a project. Many crew have asked me to tell them about future projects because they had a great experience working on set.

Though it is corny, I do feel warm and fuzzy inside when someone I have worked with tells me that I inspired them to work harder than they ever have before. When someone looks up to me as a mentor I automatically up my game. Constantly bettering yourself is both the catalyst and the result of people looking to you as their leader.

In conclusion, leadership can be defined as a state of management and control in which the leader's abilities must improve overtime though constant learning and through the execution of strategies that impact people in positive ways. Leadership transcends age and artistic talent. Being a great leader is something that anyone can do if they so choose. So make the choice.

INTERVIEW WITH
NORMAN BUCKLEY

Pretty Little Liars, Gossip Girl, The Fosters, Rizzoli & Isles, The O.C.

What does the word 'motivate' mean to you?

I'll go with Webster's definition: "to stimulate someone's interest or enthusiasm for doing something." My job is to provide a reason to the cast and crew for investing in the story we're telling.

What does 'inspire' mean to you?

It actually means to draw breath. I like the idea of breathing in creative energy, which you then exhale to others. I oftentimes find that one of the most effective directions I can offer to actors is to remind them to breathe. We inspire each other by reminding ourselves to always be present and to trust what's happening and not to feel that we have to "control" it.

Who are your inspirations and why?

I am inspired by many people. I get great inspiration from all of the department heads I work with every day. Each person brings their own type of expertise to the table and I draw upon all of it.

As far as inspirations for my directing work—I have always been a huge fan of Alfred Hitchcock, George Stevens, Federico Fellini, and Billy Wilder. I study all of these filmmakers to understand how they tell stories.

Who has motivated you over the years?

I have been motivated by my family, by my late spouse, Davyd Whaley, who was a remarkable painter, and by my friends. I have received more than my share of blessings in this life, and a fair amount of good luck.

How has their support changed you and/or your work ethic?

I owe it to those who have supported me to always do my best. I try to be single-pointed in my focus. I try to stay present.

How do you motivate and inspire your cast and crew? Explain what you say and/or do.

As I said above, I try to remind everyone I work with to be present. I ask only that they all come to play full out, and it's my hope that they'll leave their ego at the door. The filmmaking process is a miraculous one when everyone trusts the process. But when someone's ego is getting in the way, I often ask them how I can help them. If people realize that your desire is to support rather than control, then they'll often drop their own attempt to control.

How do you stay motivated and inspired on set?

I always encourage everyone to offer their best ideas. Input from other people motivates me. If I have down time during lighting setups, then I'll read or listen to music.

Have you ever had an experience where your efforts to be a motivating leader and an inspiring director resulted in something unexpected? If so, can you describe what happened?

During the first season finale of *Gossip Girl* I had a huge day in front of me. We were shooting a wedding reception scene with all of the principal cast members and it was going to be a very long day. For some mystical reason I decided to bring everyone to the set at the very beginning of the day and I described for them the entire day's work—where people would be sitting, where the cameras would be, the order of shooting, and I explained all of the blocking for all of the scenes. I wanted people to understand how much work there was, and I wanted them to understand how important it was for them to be ready when we needed them, and also why everyone was going to be needed all day long. At lunch that day I tripped on a marble staircase and shattered my nose, so I was taken to the emergency room and was unable to finish the day. However, because I had explained the plan so completely, one of the producers stepped in and was able to finish the day's work. And it was exactly as I had planned. It taught me two things: that no one is indispensable, but also that a good plan works.

What is your favourite inspiring or motivational quote?

I don't know that it's my favorite, but I like this quote: "Unless you have prepared yourself to profit by your chance, the opportunity will only make you ridiculous. A great occasion is valuable to you just in proportion as you have educated yourself to make use of it." – Orison Swett Marden

Why is it your favourite?

I believe in preparation, but I believe in also letting go and trusting fate.

Any other general advice or stories that you would like to add?

(The content below is borrowed from Norman's blog with his permission.)

A friend used to say to me "free advice is worth exactly what you pay for it, which is nothing". However, that doesn't seem to stop people from asking and I find that I say the same things over and over.

I think the most important advice I can give is this: be clear about what you want to achieve, ask yourself who has achieved that, then look for opportunities to politely approach that person or persons, tell them your goal, and ask him or her to point you in a direction.

I always tell my students that people are busy, so you want to make your request brief and something the person can accomplish for you immediately and with little effort. I cannot answer all requests on Twitter and Facebook but I'm a big believer in social media and I like the way it democratizes access. But don't abuse the access and have respect for the context.

As a director, I have a strong aesthetic point of view, and I make clear to my collaborators what I believe, but I'm also willing to change my mind if someone has a better idea. I want and desire that my collaborators tell me honestly what they think. I think it is very important to have a point of view, whatever your job. Sometimes that point of view will be welcomed, and sometimes it won't. It's important to learn to read a room, and know when to speak and when not to. When asked, be honest as to your opinions but also be kind. Everyone is doing the best they can with the material they have. Never dismiss another's point of view in a rude manner, in order to prove yourself. (In my younger days I wasn't always kind. Those moments, when I wasn't, haunt me.)

Never condescend or be dismissive of anything that you are working on. I always tell my assistants to find what they love about a job and focus on that. Being dismissive of the material, or the talent, is unacceptable. Negativity breeds inferior work.

I think it's important to always look for opportunities to learn more. Read a variety of books, go to museums, watch foreign films, see theatre, listen to music, watch everything and most of all, watch people. Be more interested in being the thing that watches and not that which is watched. Ask people what they do and what they love about their job. Be willing to learn more about that thing that doesn't interest you, just a little more anyway. If it's interesting to somebody, it's worth learning about.

It's important to hold to one's own ideas of what's right, to continue to develop one's own artistic point of view. If you're asked to do something you think is completely unacceptable, then you should be willing to leave the job.

The final most important thing to say is this: don't get discouraged and don't give up. People admire persistence and courage — they can't help but pick up on energy that is positive. And if a dream is worth having, it's worth pursuing in the face of rejection and opposition. There are many great people who are willing to encourage you along the way. Look for those people and surround yourself with them.

> **– BONUS –**
>
> Download a bonus interview with Yael Staav (*An Awesome Book of Love*).
> Visit **beyondthedirectorschair.com/bookbonus** to get access.

AFTERWORD

I'M SO GLAD I included interviews with directors who have diverse backgrounds because I learned a lot from them. I realized after writing this book that by having multiple viewpoints and interviewing people with a wide range of experiences I am being a leader because having an open mind is also a key leadership skill.

As I'm sure you have understood by reading this book, there are many elements that go into directing. While knowing a lot of technical knowledge can be an asset, it is not what will make you a great leader. There's a reason that you hire a crew that is technically adept and hire actors that are brilliant at their craft.

Go beyond the director's chair and be the leader. Do more than what is expected of you from a technical standpoint. Spend as much time practising your leadership skills as you do improving your shot lists and blocking. You will be remembered by cast and crew for your abilities as a leader equally, if not more so, for your vision and artistic merit.

Each and every experience that you have informs who you are, which ultimately determines how you decide to carry yourself and behave as a director. I do hope that this book has given you some insight to allow you to be a confident leader.

ABOUT THE AUTHOR

Award-winning author, Leah Rifkin, is the founder and CEO of Scarlet Lens Productions, and brings a passion for media and a love of storytelling to her role. Aside from honing her skills as a director, Leah has grown as an entrepreneur and producer by learning from some of the best in town.

Leah is a graduate of the acclaimed Radio & Television Arts program at Ryerson University. She has always had a gift for transforming ideas into visual stories on screen. She has created, developed, directed, and produced web series, short films, television series, and innovative projects. Leah also works with many up-and-coming screenwriters and is producing several original projects they have created.

Her strong leadership skills and creative energy served her well as the lead media instructor at the summer program of Canada's Academy of Stage and Studio Arts, where she shared her wealth of knowledge with children and youth eager to learn the craft of media.

With a strong entrepreneurial spirit at her core, Leah thrives on developing innovative work as a director, producer, and writer. She was nominated for the 2013 Digi Award for Graduate of the Year, and is the executive producer and director of the award-winning edutainment web series, *Out Of Frame*. Her short film, *The Breath*, was accepted into the 2016 Miami Independent Film Festival and the 2016 International Monthly Film Festival. Additionally, the interactive feature film script for *Revolution 10*, which Leah created and co-developed, was accepted into the 2017 Beverly Hills Film Festival.

"My greatest joy is knowing that the stories I create have a positive effect on the lives of others. Story telling is a powerful tool to innovate ideas, provide insight, and inspire minds to achieve more. My purpose is to share stories with the world."

To learn more about Scarlet Lens Productions and its original projects as well as the video work Leah does for clients please reach out and connect:

www.scarletlensproductions.com
416-839-2752
info@scarletlensproductions.com

www.ingramcontent.com/pod-product-compliance
Lightning Source LLC
LaVergne TN
LVHW051554070426
835507LV00021B/2576